Tulip Wall Hanging
pages 4 - 5

Hearts Pillows, Sachet
pages 6 - 7

Flower Pots
pages 8 - 10

Under the Sea
pages 11 - 13

Wild Flowers
pages 14 - 15

Pocket Purse
pages 16 - 17

Baby Quilt
page 18 - 19

Raining Cats & Dogs
pages 20 - 21

Sunbonnet Sue & Sam
pages 22 - 23

Hexagon Stars
pages 24 - 25, 35

Tree Skirt
pages 26 - 27

Easy Elegance
pages 28 - 31

Spring Fling Tote
pages 32 - 35

Dolls
pages 36 - 39

Loving Hearts
pages 38 - 39

Braided Toys
pages 40 -41

Monkey Purse
page 42

Holiday Ornaments
page 43

Pin Cushions
pages 44 - 45

Purr-fect Pillow
page 48

Owl Purse
page 49

Owl Pillows
pages 50 - 51

# Tulips & Mums Wall Hanging

*pieced by*
*Donna Arends Hansen*
*quilted by Edna Summers*

*Just as a bouquet of pretty flowers brightens your day, this hanging garden will brighten any place in your home. Soft vintage fabrics whisper the nostalgic memories of a time when people stopped to smell the flowers. Life was slower then.*

*Capture the essence of those times in a wall hanging that goes together at the speed of a 4G iphone. The look may be old fashioned, but the techniques are totally up to date when you use the GO! baby cutting system to prepare your pieces. It's easy, accurate and quick. Get ready, cut, sew with the baby GO!*

SIZE: 19½" x 38½"

YARDAGE:
We used *Moda* "Pom Pom de Paris"
OR use the fabric colors of your choice.

| | |
|---|---|
| Center | ⅓ yard of Light Cream |
| Applique Fabrics: | 10" x 10" of Light Red |
| Applique Fabrics: | 10" x 10" of Dark Red print |
| | 9" x 18" of Dark Green print |
| | 5" x 5" of Cream print |
| Border #1 & Cornerstones | ¼ yard of Red floral |
| Border #2 & Binding | ½ yard of Red print |
| Backing | 1 yard |
| Batting | 28" x 47" |

*Steam-a-Seam 2* fusible web for applique
*DMC* Black embroidery floss, chenille needle
Sewing machine, needle, thread

*AccuQuilt® GO! baby™* Fabric Cutter (#55300),
GO! die #55007 Round Flower - petals, center, lea, stem
GO! die #55030 Critters
GO! die #55328 Tulip

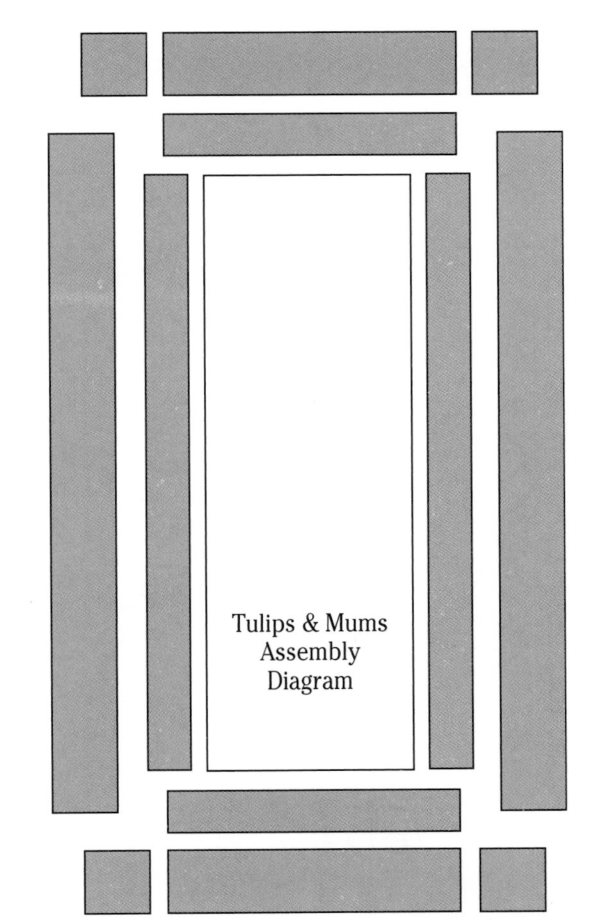


1. CENTER:
Cut the background 10" x 29".

2. BORDER #1:
Cut 2½" strips across the width of fabric.
Cut 2 strips 2½" x 29" for sides.
Cut 2 strips 2½" x 14" for the top and bottom.
Sew side borders to the quilt. Press.
Sew top and bottom borders to the quilt. Press.

3. APPLIQUES:
Apply fusible web to the back of the applique fabrics before cutting.
Cut the following applique pieces:
**#55328 Tulip:**
2 Dark Red centers, 4 Red print petals
**#55030 Critters:**
1 Dark Red butterfly wings,
1 Red print butterfly body
**#55007 Round Flower:**
8 Dark Green leaves, 9 Dark Green stems,
**Large Flower:**
1 Dark Red solid, 2 Red print
**Hexagon Flower Centers:**
1 Dark Red solid, 1 Red print,
1 Cream print
**1" Circle:**
2 Cream, 1 Red print
**Small Circle:**
1 Dark Red, 1 Red print, 1 Cream
Position applique pieces and fuse in place.
Applique as desired.
Embroider the butterfly antennae with Black floss.

4. BORDER #2:
Cut four Red floral cornerstones 3½" x 3½".
Cut 3½" strips of Red print across the width of fabric.
Cut 2 strips 3½" x 33" for sides.
Cut 2 strips 3½" x 14" for the top and bottom.
Sew side borders to the quilt. Press.
Sew a cornerstone to each end of the top and bottom borders. Press.
Sew top and bottom borders to the quilt. Press.

5. FINISHING:
**Quilt and Bind the edges:**
Sew 2½" strips together end to end to equal 126".

## Heart Pillows

*pieced by Donna M.J. Kinsey*

*Buzz is in the air. Are you looking for a different sort of engagement or wedding gift?*

*Something lighthearted and unique?*

*Something memorable, made by your own hand?*

*Heart pillows are perfect for Valentine's day and sachets are always really fun to make.*

## Heart Sachet

PREPARATION:

For one sachet, die cut the following:

#55029 Hearts - 2", 3", 5"

Die cut two 5" hearts from Red print

MAKE THE SACHET:

Place two 5" hearts with right sides.

Sew around the outer edge, leaving an opening for turning.

Turn right side out.

Stuff with potpourri, scented salts, or polyfil.

Stitch the opening closed.

Sew a ribbon to the heart for hanging.

## Heart Pillows

SIZE: Large: 13½" x 14"
Medium: 10½" x 11½"
Sachet: 3½" x 4"

YARDAGE:
We used *Moda* "Le Petit Poulet" by American Jane
OR use the fabric colors of your choice.
⅙ yard Red dot for background
⅙ yard Red floral for background
⅙ yard Red print for background
⅛ yard Blue print for bee body

Binding on large heart ⅓ yard Red/White check
Binding on med. heart ⅓ yard Blue print
Backing ⅚ yard
Batting 2 yards of fluffy batting
Sewing machine, needle, thread
*Steam-a-Seam 2* fusible web for appliques
Two 7" zippers
Sachet - Polyfil stuffing, handful of Potpourri, scented salts

*AccuQuilt® GO! baby*™ Fabric Cutter (#55300),
GO! die #55010 Square 5"
GO! die #55030 Critters
GO! die #55029 Hearts - 2", 3", 5"

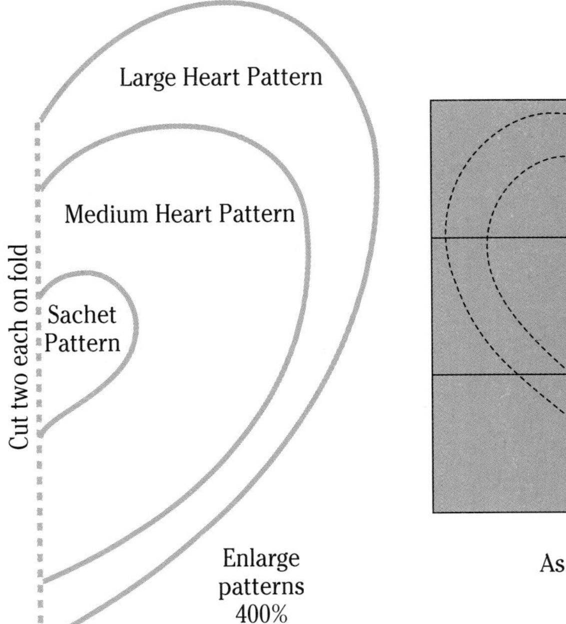

9-Patch Assembly Diagram

**The following instructions will make 2 pillows.**

PREPARATION FOR HEARTS:
For each pillow, die cut all pieces as listed below.

| **Color** | #55010 Square 5" |
|---|---|
| Red floral | 2 |
| Red print | 2 |
| Red dots | 5 |

PREPARATION FOR APPLIQUES:
Apply fusible web to the back of applique fabrics.
Die cut all pieces as listed below.

| **Color** | #55030 Critters |
|---|---|
| Blue print | 2 bee bodies |
| Red/White check | 2 sets of bee wings |

9-PATCH PILLOWS:
For each pillow, arrange 3 rows of 3 blocks each. Press.
Sew the rows together.
Cut the piece into a heart shape.

APPLIQUES:
Position the bees in place.
Applique as desired.

**Quilting:**
Using the heart as the pattern, cut out a batting and a backing. Layer and quilt as desired.

CONSTRUCT THE PILLOW:
Using the heart as the pattern, cut out a pillow back.
Cut the pillow back in half. Sew a seam leaving 7" open in the center. Sew a zipper in place.
With wrong sides together, sew the front to the back.

Medium Heart Pillow

Large Heart Pillow

**Binding:**
Measure a 12" x 12" square of fabric.
Cut on one diagonal to establish the bias.
Cut 2" strips on the bias and sew together end to end.
You need 46" for the large pillow and 40" for the medium pillow.
Sew binding around the outer edge.

FINISH:
Unzip the back of the pillow. Stuff with 4 layers of fluffy batting.
Close the zipper.

# Flower Pots Wall Hanging

*by Donna Arends Hansen*
*quilted by Sue Needle*

*Every windowsill needs a potted plant and this wall hanging offers a selection worthy of a garden center.*

*Plant your garden in your favorite flower colors and don't forget the butterfly - he's coming to sip the nectar of your creativity.*

*This little project should be a top seller at the town fair or hospital fund raiser.*

SIZE: 22" x 30"

YARDAGE:

We used *Moda* "Oasis" by 3 sisters
OR use the fabric colors of your choice.

- 1/4 yard Cream print
- 1/4 yard Cream with small print
- 1/4 yard Cream with medium print
- 9" x 10" of Light Green
- 12" x 12" of Red/Pink large print
- 12" x 16" of Pink small print

| | |
|---|---|
| Border #1, Pots, & Flowers | 1/4 yard Red floral |
| Border #2 & Binding | 3/4 yard Cream print |
| Backing | 1 yard |
| Batting | 32" x 38" |

*Steam-a-Seam 2* fusible web for appliques
Sewing machine, needle, thread

*AccuQuilt® GO! baby™* Fabric Cutter (#55300),
- GO! die #55015 Tumbler 3½"
- GO! die #55014 Strip Cutter 2½"
- GO! die #55030 Critters
- GO! die #55331 Stems & Leaves
- GO! die #55327 Daisy
- GO! die #55007 Round Flower
- GO! die #55042 Funky Flower
- GO! die #55012 Circles - 2", 3", 5"

PREPARATION FOR CENTER BACKGROUND:
Die cut all pieces as listed below.

| **Color** | #55015 Tumbler 3½" |
|---|---|
| Cream small print | 8 |
| Cream medium print | 6 |
| Cream print | 8 |
| Red floral | 6 |

| **Color** | #55014 Strip Cutter 2½" |
|---|---|
| Cream small print | cut 2 strips, each 2½" x 14½" |
| Cream medium print | cut 2 strips, each 2½" x 14½" |
| Cream print | cut 1 strip 2½" x 14½" |

PREPARATION FOR APPLIQUES:
Apply fusible web to the back of fabrics before cutting.
Die cut all pieces as listed below.
Sort the pieces into groups for each flower.

| **Color** | #55030 Critters |
|---|---|
| Red/Pink | 1 butterfly wing |
| Pink print | 1 butterfly body |

| **Color** | #55331 Stems & Leaves |
|---|---|
| Light Green | 6 straight stems (1 per flower) |
| | 12 leaves (6 in reverse) |

| **Color** | #55327 Daisy |
|---|---|
| Pink print | 13 small petals for Flower #2 |
| | 12 small petals for Flower #5 |

| **Color** | #55007 Round Flower |
|---|---|
| Pink print | 4 small circles (1 each for Flowers #2, 3, 5, 6) |
| | 1 large circle (1") for Flower #4 |
| | 2 large flowers (1 each for Flowers #3, 4) |
| | 1 hexagon center for Flower #6 |
| Red/Pink | 2 large flowers (1 each for Flowers #1, 6) |
| Red Floral | 2 small circles (1 each for Flowers #1, 4) |
| | 1 hexagon center for Flower #4 |
| | 3 large 1" circles (1 each for Flowers #2, 5, 6) |

| **Color** | #55042 Funky Flower |
|---|---|
| Pink print | 1 center for Flower #1 |
| Red/Pink | 1 center for Flower #3 |

| **Color** | #55012 Circle 2", 3", 5" |
|---|---|
| Red/Pink | 1 circle (2") for Flower #4 |
| Red Floral | 2 circles (2") (1 each for Flowers #1, 3) |

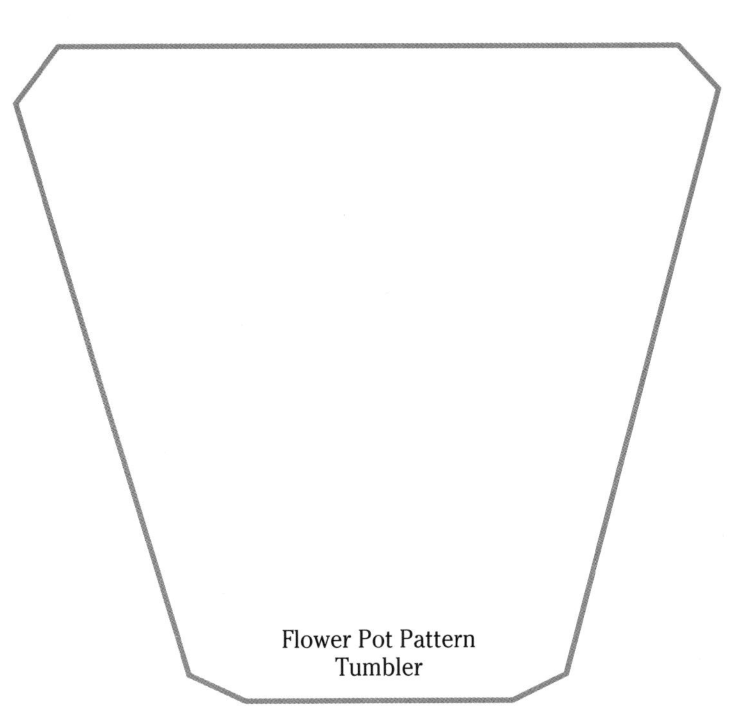
Flower Pot Pattern
Tumbler

ASSEMBLY:
Refer to the Assembly Diagram.
Arrange the pieces on a work surface.
There are 4 rows of tumblers with 7 per row.

**Rows 1 & 3:**
Sew 7 assorted Cream pieces. Press.

**Rows 2 & 4:**
Sew Cream - Red - Cream - Red - Cream - Red - Cream. Press.
Trim each row to 14½".

continued on page 10

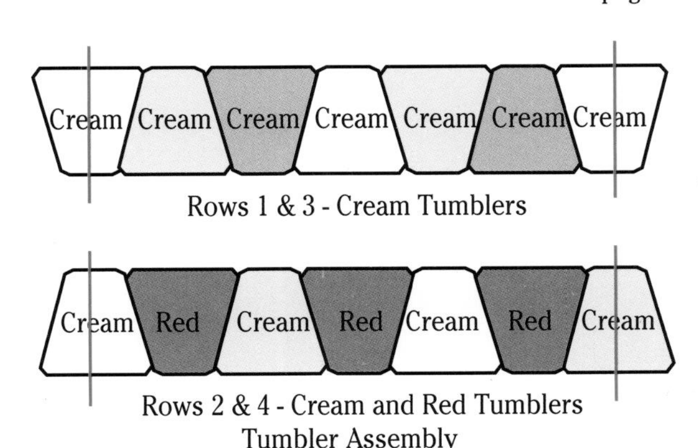

Rows 1 & 3 - Cream Tumblers
Rows 2 & 4 - Cream and Red Tumblers
Tumbler Assembly

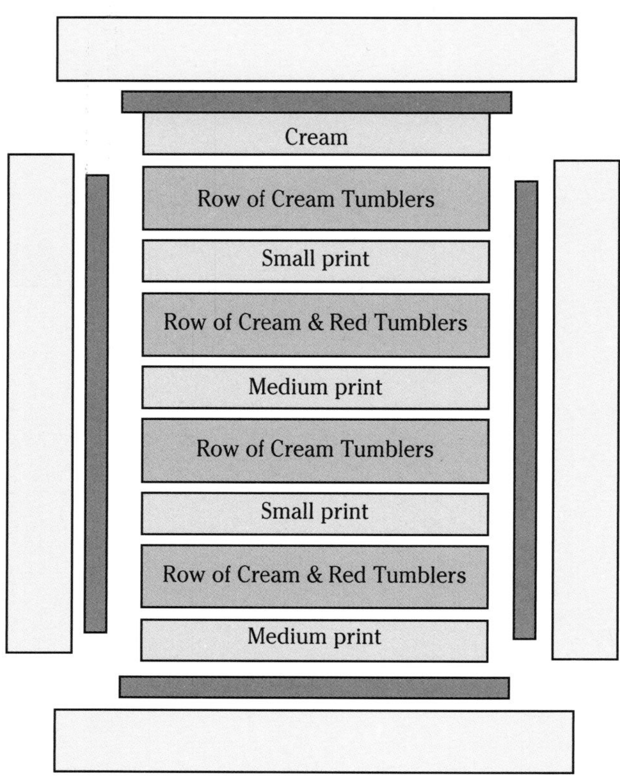


Assembly Diagram

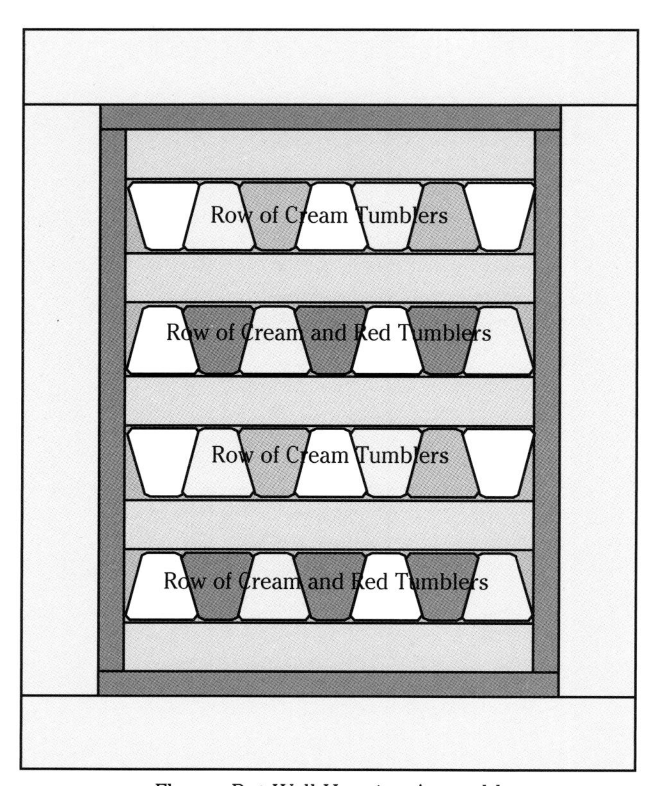


Flower Pot Wall Hanging Assembly

continued from page 9

ASSEMBLE THE QUILT:

Arrange the rows and sashing strips on a work surface.
Sew the rows together. Press.

**Border #1:**

Cut 2 strips $1\frac{1}{2}$"x $22\frac{1}{2}$" for sides.
Cut 2 strips $1\frac{1}{2}$" x $16\frac{1}{2}$" for top and bottom.
Sew side borders to the quilt. Press.
Sew top and bottom borders to the quilt. Press.

**Border #2:**

Cut 2 strips $3\frac{1}{2}$"x $24\frac{1}{2}$" for sides.
Cut 2 strips $3\frac{1}{2}$" x $22\frac{1}{2}$" for top and bottom.
Sew side borders to the quilt. Press.
Sew top and bottom borders to the quilt. Press.

APPLIQUES:

Position and press the appliques in place.
Applique as desired.

**Quilt and Bind the edges:**

Sew $2\frac{1}{2}$" strips together end to end to equal 114".

Applique flowers, stems, leaves and the butterfly

continued from pages 12 - 13

**Medium Goldfish E:**

Use a Dark Orange 3" circle for the body.
Cut a Light Orange 3" circle in half for the tail.
Cut a Light Orange 2" circle in half for the fins.

**Octopus F:**

Use a Dark Blue 5" circle for the body.
Cut a Light Blue 3" wedge in half for eyes.
Use 4 Light Blue and 4 Dark Blue stems for arms.

**Starfish, Seaweed, & Kelp:**

Position stems, leaves and starfish.
Applique as desired.
Sew buttons in place for eyes, nose, and mouth.

BORDER #1:

Cut 2 strips 1½" x 20½" for sides.
Cut 2 strips 1½" x 22½" for the top and bottom.
Sew side borders to the quilt. Press.
Sew top and bottom borders to the quilt. Press.

4. BORDER #2:

Sides - Sew the following rectangles together vertically to make strips 3½" x 22½":
A - B - A - B - A. Press. Make 2.

Top & Bottom - Sew the following rectangles together horizontally to make strips 3½" x 22½":
C - A - B - A - B - A - C. Press. Make 2.

Sew a side border to each side of the quilt. Press.
Sew the top and bottom borders to the quilt. Press.

FINISHING:

**Quilt and Bind the edges:**

Sew 2½" strips together end to end to equal 122".

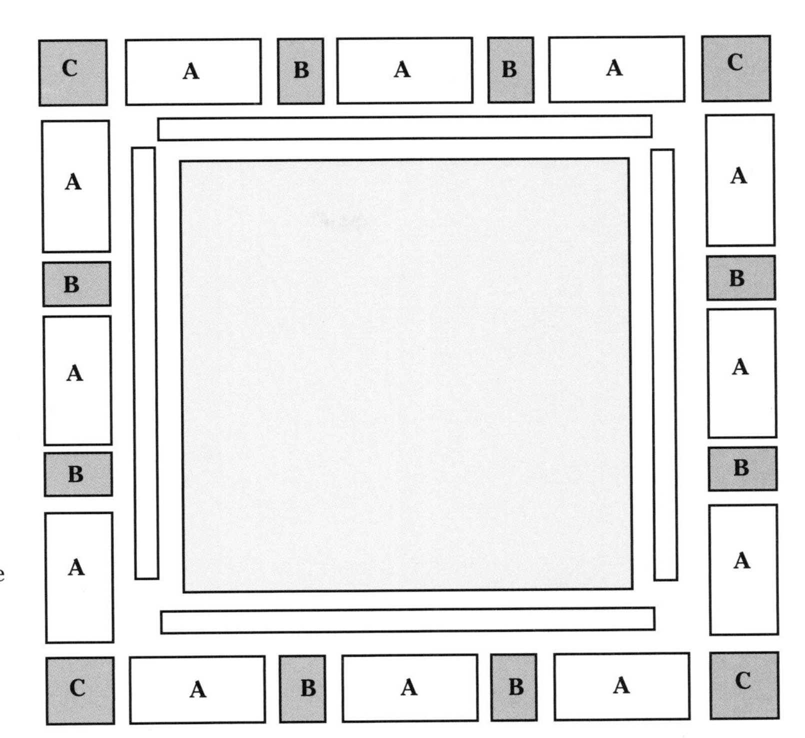


Under the Sea Wall Hanging Assembly

# Under the Sea Wall Hanging

*pieced by Donna M.J. Kinsey*
*quilted by Osie Lebowitz*

*Dive into your stash and create your own undersea adventure. Strands of kelp swish lazily amidst the goldfish, bluegill and friendly octopus.*

SIZE: 28" x 28"
YARDAGE:
We used *Moda* "Fresh" and fabrics from our stash
OR use the fabric colors of your choice.

| | |
|---|---|
| Applique Fabrics: | 1/3 yard of Dark Blue<br>Dark Orange print 5" x 5"<br>Light Orange print 5" x 8" |
| Center | 2/3 yard of White print |
| Border #1 & Seaweed | 1/4 yard of Green print |
| Border #2, Appliques & Binding | 1/2 yard of Light Blue print |
| Border #2 | 1/4 yard of White paisley |
| Backing | 1 yard |
| Batting | 38" x 38" |

*Steam-a-Seam 2* fusible web for appliques
Assorted buttons
Sewing machine, needle, thread

*AccuQuilt® GO! baby*™ Fabric Cutter (#55300),
GO! die #55014 Strip Cutter 2 1/2"
GO! die #55005 Rectangle 3 1/2" x 6 1/2"
GO! die #55006 Square 3 1/2"
GO! die #55012 Circles - 2", 3", 5"
GO! die #55331 Stems & Leaves
GO! die #55334 Fun Flower

PREPARATION FOR BORDER #2:
Die cut all pieces as listed below.

| **Color** | #55005 Rectangle 3 1/2" x 6 1/2" |
|---|---|
| White paisley | 12 rectangles (**A**) |
| **Color** | #55006 Square 3 1/2" |
| Light Blue | 4 cornerstones (**C**) |
| **Color** | #55014 Strip Cutter 2 1/2" |
| Light Blue | cut a strip 2 1/2" x 30"<br>cut into 8 rectangles 2 1/2" x 3 1/2" (**B**) |

PREPARATION FOR APPLIQUES:
Apply fusible web to the back of fabrics before cutting.

| **Color** | #55012 Circle 2", 3", 5" |
|---|---|
| Light Orange | 1 circle 2", 1 circle 3" |
| Dark Orange | 1 circle 3" |
| Light Blue | 4 circles 2", 2 circles 3", 1 circle 5" |
| Dark Blue | 3 circles 2", 1 circle 3", 2 circles 5" |

| **Color** | #55334 Fun Flower |
|---|---|
| Dark Blue | 1 for starfish |

| **Color** | #55331 Stems & Leaves |
|---|---|
| **Octopus Arms:** | |
| Light Blue | 7 leaves, 4 stems (2 in reverse) |
| Dark Blue | 2 leaves, 4 stems (2 in reverse) |
| Green | 8 stems for seaweed |

Assembly Diagram

CENTER:
Cut the background 20 1/2" x 20 1/2".

APPLIQUES:
Position applique pieces.
Fuse in place as follows:

**Large Blue Fish A:**
Use a Dark Blue 5" circle for the body.
Cut a Light Blue 5" circle in half for the tail.
Cut a Light Blue 3" circle in half for the fins.
Cut a Light Blue wedge for the eye.

**Medium Blue Fish B:**
Use a Light Blue 3" circle for the body.
Cut a Dark Blue 3" circle in half for the tail.
Cut a Dark Blue 2" circle in half for the fins.

**Small Blue Fish C & D:**
Use a Dark Blue 2" circle for the body.
Cut a Light Blue 2" circle in half for the tail.
Cut another Light Blue 2" circle into 8 wedges.
Use 2 wedges for fins.

continued on page 11

# Wild Flowers Table Runner

*pieced and quilted by Donna Arends Hansen*

*A garden of quilted flowers dance across your table as your guests anticipate a creative presentation. Nothing spices up a family meal or a potluck like a beautifully appointed table.*

*Flowers never go out of style and they complement every decor. Choose your favorite colors and have fun with flowers.*

SIZE: 12" x 48"

YARDAGE:

We used *Moda* "Lovely" by Sandy Gervais
OR use the fabric colors of your choice.

- ⅜ yard White for background
- ⅜ yard White print for background
- 10" x 10" scrap of Red print for flowers
- 10" x 16" scrap of Turquoise for stems
- 10" x 17" scrap of Red for flowers & pots

| | |
|---|---|
| Binding, Leaves & Centers | ½ yard Turquoise print |
| Backing | 1⅛ yards |
| Batting | 20" x 56" |

*Steam-a-Seam 2* fusible web for appliques
Sewing machine, needle, thread

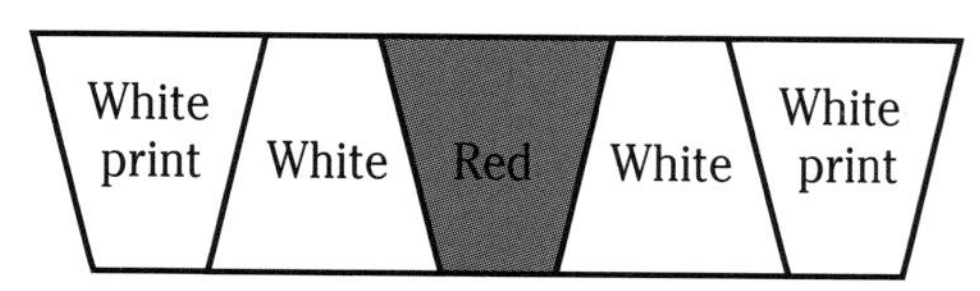


Tumbler Strip
Make 2

*AccuQuilt® GO! baby™* Fabric Cutter (#55300),
GO! die #55015 Tumbler 3½"
GO! die #55014 Strip Cutter 2½"
GO! die ##55331 Stems & Leaves
GO! die #55042 Funky Flower

PREPARATION FOR CENTER BACKGROUND:
Die cut all pieces as listed below.
Center Strips 2½" x 42½"

| **Color** | #55014 Strip Cutter 2½" |
|---|---|
| White solid | 3 |
| White print | 3 |

Tumbler Piecess for End Strips:

| **Color** | #55015 Tumbler 3½" |
|---|---|
| White solid | 4 |
| White print | 4 |
| Red solid | 2 |

PREPARATION FOR APPLIQUES:
Apply fusible web to the back of applique fabrics before cutting.

| **Color** | #55031 Stems & Leaves |
|---|---|
| Turquoise | 2 straight stem sets (1 per end) |
| Turquoise | 20 leaves (10 in reverse) |

| **Color** | #55042 Funky Flower |
|---|---|
| Red | 4 large flowers, 2 small flowers, 1 circle center |
| Red | 4 large flowers, 2 small flowers, 7 circle centers |
| Turq. print | 8 small flowers, 4 circle centers |

CENTER:
Sew the 6 White 2½" x 42½" strips together along the long sides. Alternate the colors to make a piece 12½" x 42½". Press.

ENDS:
Refer to the Tumbler Strip diagram.
Sew 5 tumblers together with the Red tumbler in the center forming a flower pot. Press.
Make 2, one for each end of the table runner and set aside.
You will sew the Tumbler Strips to the runner after the applique is finished so you catch the ends of the stems in the seam.

APPLIQUES:
Fuse appliques in place.
Applique as desired.

ASSEMBLY:
Sew a tumbler strip to each end of the runner. Press.

FINISHING:
**Quilt and Bind the edges:**
Sew 2½" turquoise strips together end to end to equal 130".

Wild Flowers Table Runner
Assembly Diagram

# Pocket Purse

*pieced by Donna M.J. Kinsey*

*I love purses with compartments and this purse fills the bill.*

*The outer pocket makes it easy to reach the cell phone, handkerchief, and other essentials while the zipper compartment is roomy enough to safely stow your wallet, money, and car keys.*

*This pocket purse allows you to travel light and with distinction. Nobody is going to have one exactly like yours.*

SIZE: 5½" x 8½"

YARDAGE:
We used *Moda* "Le Petit Poulet" by American Jane
OR use the fabric colors of your choice.
1 Fat quarter of Red dot for background
1 Fat quarter of Red print for background
5" x 7" of Blue print for bee body
1 Fat quarter of Red/Whitecheck for lining & wings
6" zipper
36" of Red cord for handle
*Steam-a-Seam 2* fusible web for appliques
Sewing machine, needle, thread
*AccuQuilt® GO! baby™* Fabric Cutter (#55300),
GO! die #55006 Square 3½"
GO! die #55030 Critters
GO! die ##55012 Circles - 2", 3", 5"

PREPARATION FOR PURSE FRONT AND BACK:
Die cut all pieces as listed below.

| **Color** | #55006 Square 3½" |
|---|---|
| Red dot | 9 |
| Red print | 9 |

PREPARATION FOR APPLIQUES:
Apply fusible web to the back of applique fabrics before cutting.

| **Color** | #55030 Critters |
|---|---|
| Blue print | 1 bee body |
| Red/White check | 1 bee wings |

LINING:

**Lining -**

Cut 3 check rectangles, each $6\frac{1}{2}$" x $9\frac{1}{2}$"
(1 for the pocket lining, 2 for lining inside the purse).

**Purse - Pieced Sections -**

Sew 6 Red $3\frac{1}{2}$" squares together in a rectangle.
Alternate the prints. Press. Make 2.

APPLIQUES:

Fuse the bee and wings to the purse back.
Applique as desired.

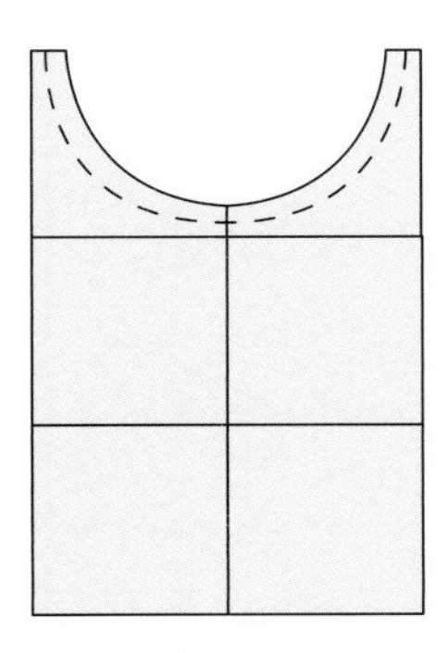

Diagram 1

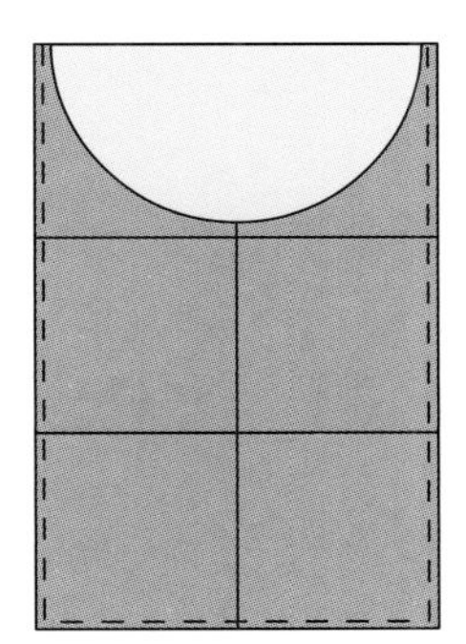

Diagram 2

PURSE POCKET:

**Cut Pocket Shape with the Circle Die:**

Place 1 pieced Purse section and 1 lining with right sides together.
Position the top portion of these layers on half of the 5" circle on the circle die.
Cut a semicircle for the top of the pocket (diagram 1).

**Sew Pocket Together:**

Sew the top semicircle of the 2 pieces with right sides together. Clip the curve.
Turn the pocket right side out.
Press.
Topstitch around the semicircle.

**Position Pocket on Purse:**

Place the pocket on top of one $6\frac{1}{2}$" x $9\frac{1}{2}$" check fabric on the table with the right sides facing you (diagram 2 - both are right side up.)
Edge stitch $\frac{1}{8}$" along the sides and bottom to hold the pocket to the purse side.

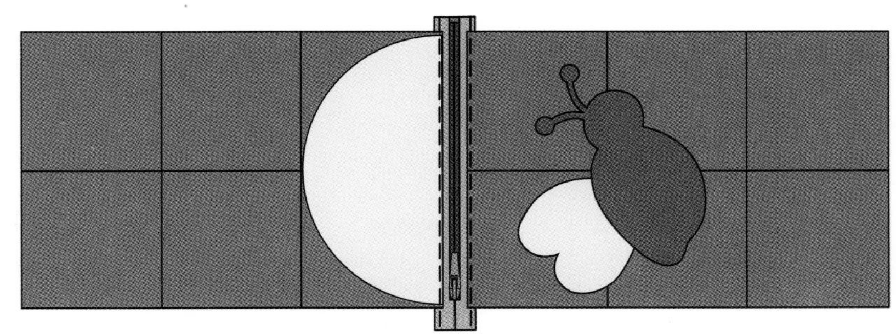

PURSE ASSEMBLY:

**Insert a Zipper:**

Lay both purse sides out flat. Turn the top edges under $\frac{1}{2}$". Press.
Sew a zipper to the top edges. Open the zipper.

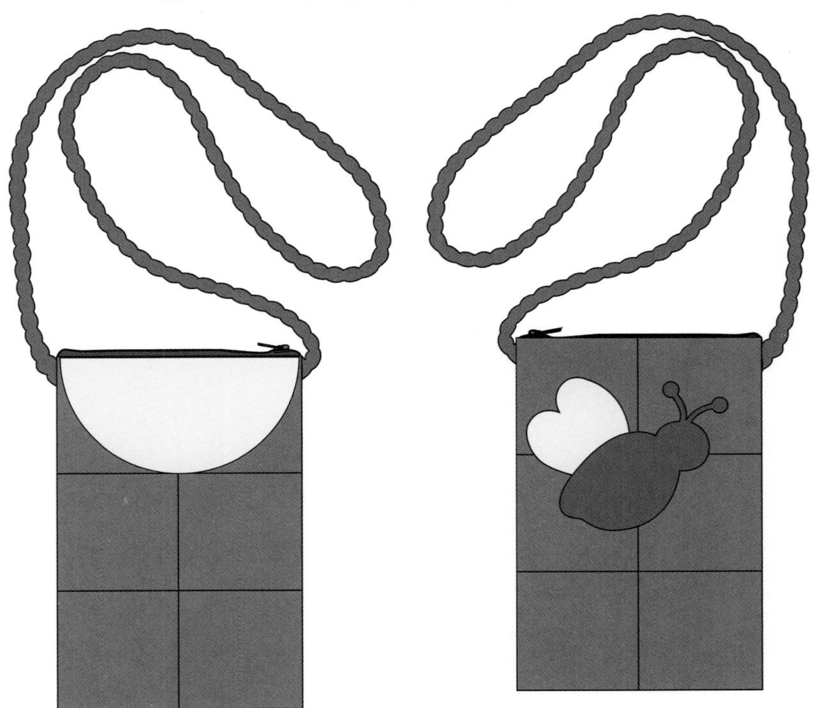

INSERT HANDLES:

Pin one end of a handle to each side of the front of purse.
Position the front and back with the right sides together.
Sew the sides and bottom of the purse, stitching securely over the handles.
Turn the purse right side out.

LINING:

With right sides together, sew the sides and bottom of lining.
Press under a $\frac{1}{2}$" hem at the top.
Slide lining into purse. Hand sew the lining around the top.

# Baby Quilt

*pieced & quilted by Osie Lebowitz*

*Has your guild or sewing circle been searching for a fabulous and fast charity quilt?*

*Look no further. Using the GO!baby cutting system, you can cut out all the pieces for this quilt in less than 15 minutes, making it possible to sew more quilts.*

*Welcome the newest family member with this wonderful quilt and create an heirloom that will be treasured for generations to come.*

*Get GOing today.*

SIZE: 28" x 32½"

YARDAGE:

We used *Moda* "Lovely" by Sandy Gervais
OR use the fabric colors of your choice.
⅓ yard White dots to cut 10 squares
⅓ yard White print to cut 10 squares
⅙ yard Turquoise solid for appliques
4" x 13" Red for apple and hearts
8" x 8" Gold for bear and duck
6" x 6" Dark Brown for bear
2" x 6" Yellow for butterfly body

| | |
|---|---|
| Border #1 & cornerstones | ¼ yard Red print |
| Border #2 & Binding | ⅚ yard Turquoise print |
| Backing | 1 yard |
| Batting | 36" x 41" |

*DMC* Black embroidery floss, chenille needle
*Steam-a-Seam 2* fusible web for appliques
Sewing machine, needle, thread

*AccuQuilt® GO! baby*™ Fabric Cutter (#55300),
GO! die #55010 Square 5"
GO! die #55030 Critters
GO! die #55012 Circles - 2", 3", 5"
GO! die #55035 Alpha Baby
GO! die #55037 Baby, Baby
GO! die #55029 Hearts - 2", 3" 4"
GO! die #55331 Stems & Leaves

PREPARATION FOR QUILT CENTER:

Die cut all pieces as listed below.

| **Color** | #55010 Square 5" |
|---|---|
| White dots | 10 |
| White print | 10 |

PREPARATION FOR APPLIQUES:

Apply fusible web to the back of fabrics before cutting.

| **Color** | #55030 Critters |
|---|---|
| Turquoise solid | 1 butterfly wings |
| Yellow | 1 butterfly body |
| **Color** | #55012 Circle 3" |
| Red solid | 1 for peach |
| **Color** | #55035 Alpha Baby |
| Turquoise solid | letters B, A, B, Y |
| **Color** | #55037 Baby, Baby |
| Gold | 1 duck, 2 bear ears, 2 bear eyebrows, 4 paw pads |
| Turquoise | 1 duck eye, 1 duck wing, 2 bear eyes, 1 bear nose, 1 bowtie |
| Dark Brown | 1 bear |
| Red | 1 duck bill |
| **Color** | ##55029 Heart 3" |
| Red | 2 hearts |
| **Color** | #55331 Stems & Leaves |
| Turquoise solid | 2 leaves for peach |
| Dark Brown | 1 stem for peach |

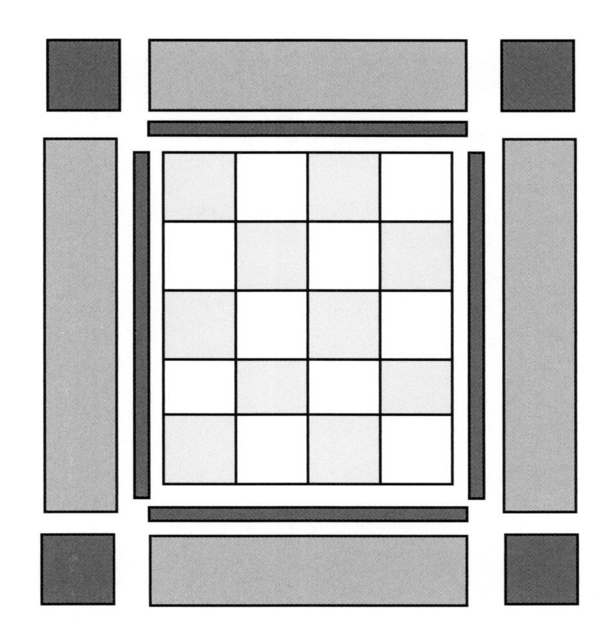

Baby Mini Quilt
Assembly Diagram

ASSEMBLY:

Refer to the Assembly Diagram.
Arrange the pieces on a work surface.
Arrange 5 rows of 4 squares each, alternating the prints. Press.
Sew the rows together. Press.

APPLIQUES:

Press the appliques onto their background squares.
Applique as desired. Embroider antennae on the butterfly.

**Border #1:**

Cut 2 strips 1½"x 23" for sides.
Cut 2 strips 1½" x 20½" for top and bottom.
Sew side borders to the quilt. Press.
Sew top and bottom borders to the quilt. Press.

**Border #2:**

Cut 2 strips 4½" x 25" for sides.
Cut 2 strips 4½" x 20½" for top and bottom.
Cut 4 Red print cornerstones 4½" x 4½". Sew 1 to each end of the top & bottom strips.
Sew side borders to the quilt. Press.
Sew top and bottom borders to the quilt. Press.

FINISHING:

**Quilt and Bind the edges:**

Sew 2½" strips together end to end to equal 132".

# It's Raining Cats and Dogs

## A Version of 'Rob Peter to Pay Paul'

*pieced by Donna Arends Hansen*
*quilted by Sue Needle*

*Here's a creative way to use both the positive and negative piece when die cutting squares of fabric.*

*For example, after cutting out the dog from a square of black, we appliqued the "hole" over the red square, so a red dog becomes visible.*

SIZE: $32\frac{1}{2}$" x $41\frac{1}{2}$"

YARDAGE:

We used *Moda* "Full Circle" by Kathy Schmitz OR use the fabric colors of your choice.

- $\frac{1}{2}$ yard to cut 17 Red squares
- $\frac{1}{3}$ yard to cut 13 Black squares
- $\frac{1}{3}$ yard to cut 12 Tan squares

| | |
|---|---|
| Border #1 | $\frac{1}{4}$ yard Black |
| Border #2 & Binding | 1 yard Red |
| Backing | $1\frac{1}{2}$ yards |
| Batting | 41" x 50" |

*Steam-a-Seam 2* fusible web for appliques
Sewing machine, needle, thread

*TIP: Mark the center of the dog and cat on the die using a White permanent paint pen. Align the center of the square with the center of the shape.*

*AccuQuilt® GO! baby*™ Fabric Cutter (#55300),
GO! die #55065 Calico Cat
GO! die #55064 Gingham Dog
GO! die #55010 Square 5"

PREPARATION FOR QUILT CENTER:
Die cut all pieces as listed below.

| **Color** | #55010 Square 5" |
|---|---|
| Red | 17 |
| Black | 13 |
| Tan | 12 |

PREPARATION FOR APPLIQUES:
Choose 2 Black and 5 Red squares.
Apply fusible web to the back of each square.
Cut out the following shapes.

| **Color** | #55065 Calico Cat |
|---|---|
| Black | 1 |
| Red | 2 |
| **Color** | #55064 Gingham Dog |
| Black | 1 |
| Red | 3 |

Raining Cats and Dogs
Assembly Diagram

1. Die cut a shape from a square.

2. Place this square (with a hole) on a second square. Applique in place.

3. Use the cut out shape.

4. Place the shape on top of a third square. Applique in place.

## A Version of 'Rob Peter to Pay Paul'

APPLIQUE and ASSEMBLY:
Arrange 7 rows of 5 squares each on a work surface.
Press the applique pieces onto their background squares.
Applique as desired.
Sew the squares together. Press.

**Border #1:**
Cut 2 strips $1\frac{1}{2}$"x 32" for sides.
Cut 2 strips $1\frac{1}{2}$" x 25" for top and bottom.
Sew side borders to the quilt. Press.
Sew top and bottom borders to the quilt. Press.

**Border #2:**
Cut 2 strips $4\frac{1}{2}$"x 34" for sides.
Cut 2 strips $4\frac{1}{2}$" x 33" for top and bottom.
Sew side borders to the quilt. Press.
Sew top and bottom borders to the quilt. Press.

FINISHING:
**Quilt and Bind the edges:**
Sew $2\frac{1}{2}$" strips together end to end to equal 160".

# Sunbonnet Sue & Sam

*pieced and quilted by Edna Summers*

*Sunbonnet Sue and Overall Sam are on parade. Dressed in their Sunday best, this group is probably on its way to a picnic, or perhaps they are standing in line for tickets at the quilt show.*

*Show off your sewing skills and love for these traditional motifs in a wall hanging that will bring a smile to your face every day.*

SIZE: 22" x 41"

YARDAGE:

We used *Moda* "Hoopla" collection OR use the fabric colors of your choice.

- 1/3 yard White for background
- 1/6 yard Blue print
- 1/6 yard Green print
- 2" x 8" of Peach solid for hands

| | |
|---|---|
| Border #2 & Appliques | 1/3 yard Green/Blue stripe |
| Border #3, Binding & Appliques | 5/6 yard Blue dots |
| Backing | 1½ yards |
| Batting | 30" x 49" |

*Steam-a-Seam 2* fusible web for appliques

Sewing machine, needle, thread

*AccuQuilt® GO! baby*™ Fabric Cutter (#55300),
GO! die #55061 Sunbonnet Sue
GO! die #55062 Overall Sam

CENTER:

Cut a White background 9½" x 32½".

APPLIQUES:

Apply fusible web to the wrong side of applique fabrics before cutting.

Using GO! die #55061 Sunbonnet Sue, cut the following pieces:

**Blue print:**
2 hats, 1 dress, 2 sleeves

**Blue dot:**
3 shoes

**Green floral:**
2 dresses, 1 hat, 1 sleeve

**Peach solid:**
3 hands

Using GO! die #55062 Overall Sam, cut the following pieces:

**Blue print:** 2 shirts
**Blue dot:** 2 shoes, 2 hats
**Green floral:** 2 suspenders
**Peach solid:** 2 hands
**Stripe:** 2 sleeves, 2 pants

Fuse appliques in place.
Applique as desired.

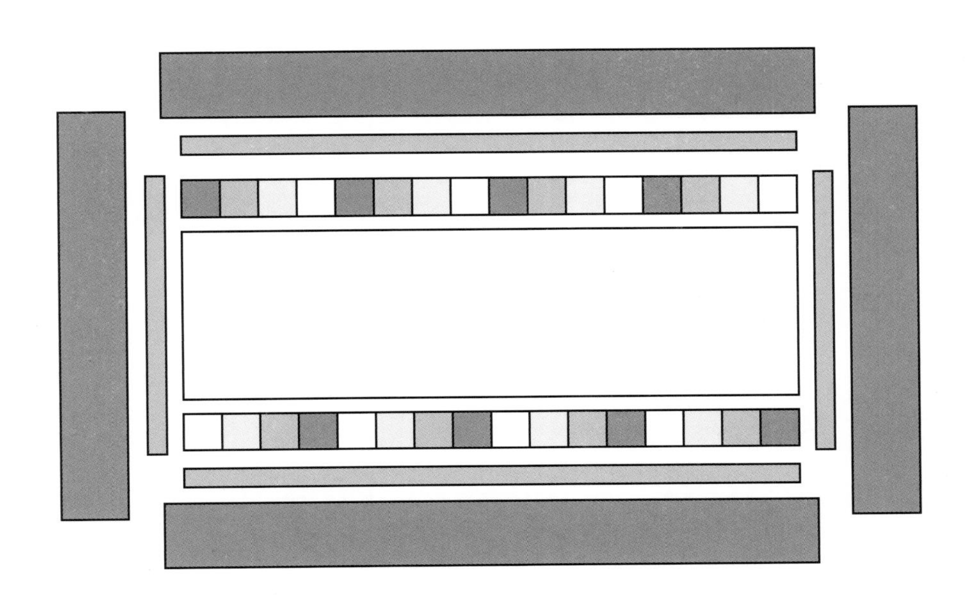

ASSEMBLY:

**Border #1:**

Cut 8 squares 2½" x 2½" of each of the following fabrics:
8 Blue dots
8 Stripe
8 Blue floral
8 Green floral

Sew 2 strips of 16 squares each (32½" long). Press.

Sew a strip to each long side of the quilt. Press.

**Border #2:**

Cut 2 strips 1½" x 32½" for the long sides.
Cut 2 strips 1½" x 15½" for the short sides.
Sew the long sides to the quilt. Press.
Sew the short sides to the quilt. Press.

**Border #3:**

Cut 2 strips 4" x 34½" for the long sides.
Cut 2 strips 4" x 22½" for the short sides.
Sew side borders to the quilt. Press.
Sew top and bottom borders to the quilt. Press.

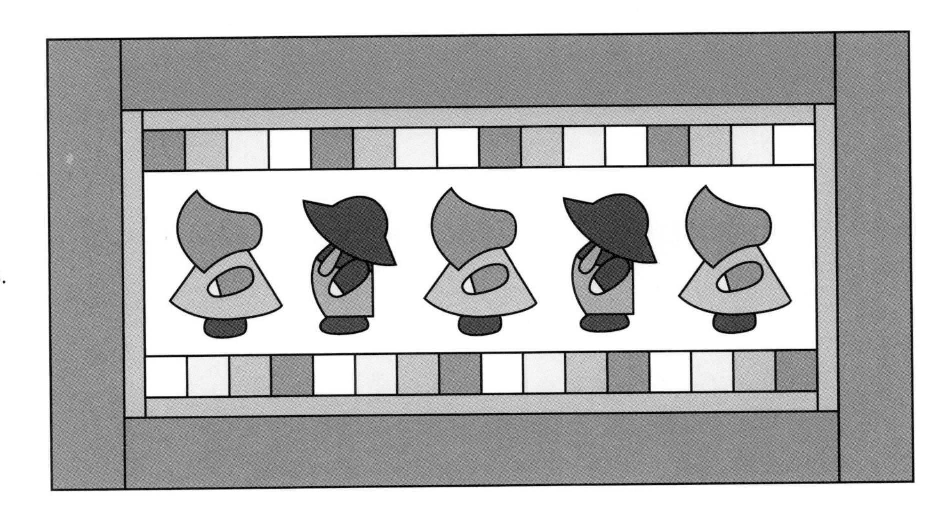

FINISHING:

**Quilt and Bind the edges:**

Sew 2½" strips together end to end to equal 136".

# Hexagon Stars

*pieced by Donna Arends Hansen*
*quilted by Sue Needle*

***The stars at night are big and bright... and they shine all day too on this amazing and easy-to-assemble quilt. If you have never tried hexagons before, go for it!***

SIZE: $35\frac{1}{2}$" x 40"

YARDAGE:
We used *Moda* "Le Petit Poulet" by American Jane
OR use the fabric colors of your choice.
1¼ yards Red print for Hexagons and Cornerstones
1 yard of Red dot for Hexagons and Binding
¾ yard of Blue print for Triangles

Border 1¼ yards of Red print
Backing 1¼ yards
Batting 44" x 48"
Sewing machine, needle, thread

*AccuQuilt® GO! baby*™ Fabric Cutter (#55300),
GO! die #55011 Hexagons - 2", 3", 5"
GO! die #55079 Equilateral Triangles

PREPARATION:
Die cut all pieces as listed below:

| | | |
|---|---|---|
| Blue print | 'C' | 114 of 2" Triangles |
| Red print | 'A-1' & 'A-2' | 28 of 5" Hexagons |
| Red dot | 'B-2' | 30 of 5" Hexagons |

PREPARE THE HEXAGONS:

**Hexagon A-1:**
Sew a triangle to 1 edge of each hexagon. Press.
Make 8 - Red print.

**Hexagon A-2:**
Sew a triangle to 2 edges of each hexagon. Press.
Make 20 - Red print.

**Hexagon B-2:**
Sew a triangle to 2 edges of each hexagon. Press.
Make 30 - Red dot.

**Triangle C:**
See below - sew to ends of Short Rows.

MAKE THE ROWS:

**Long Rows -**
**Diagram 1 -** Note: Turn the last 'A-1' to match the diagram.
Sew A-1, A-2, A-2, A-2, A-2, A-2, A-1. Press. Make 4.

**Short Rows -**
**Diagram 2 -** Sew B-2, B-2, B-2, B-2, B-2, B-2. Press. Make 5.
**Diagram 3 -** Sew 1 triangle to each end of all Short Rows. Press.

continued on page 35

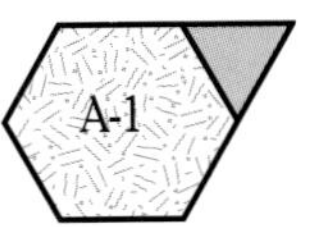

Hexagon A-1
Make 8
Red print

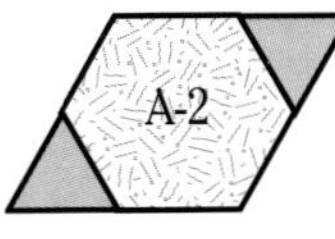

Hexagon A-2
Make 20
Red print

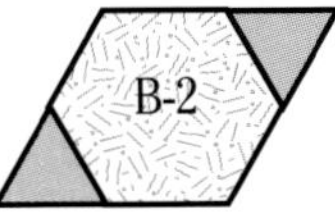

Hexagon B-2
Make 30
Red dot

Triangle C
Add 10
Blue print

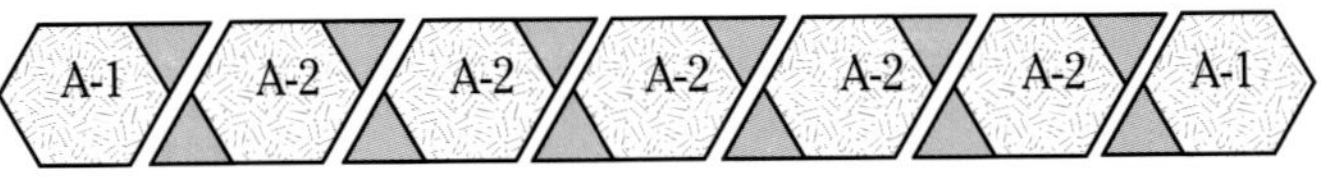

Diagram 1 - Long Rows - Red print - Make 4

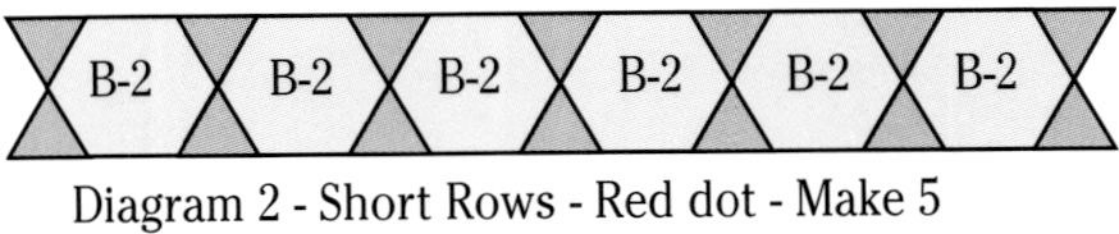

Diagram 2 - Short Rows - Red dot - Make 5

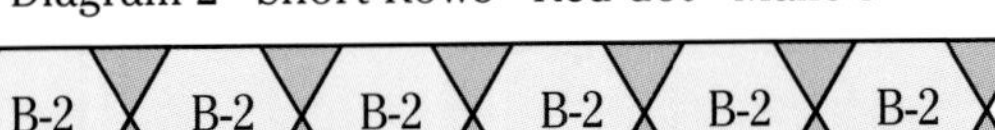

Diagram 3 - Short Rows - Add 2 of 'C' Triangles to all 5

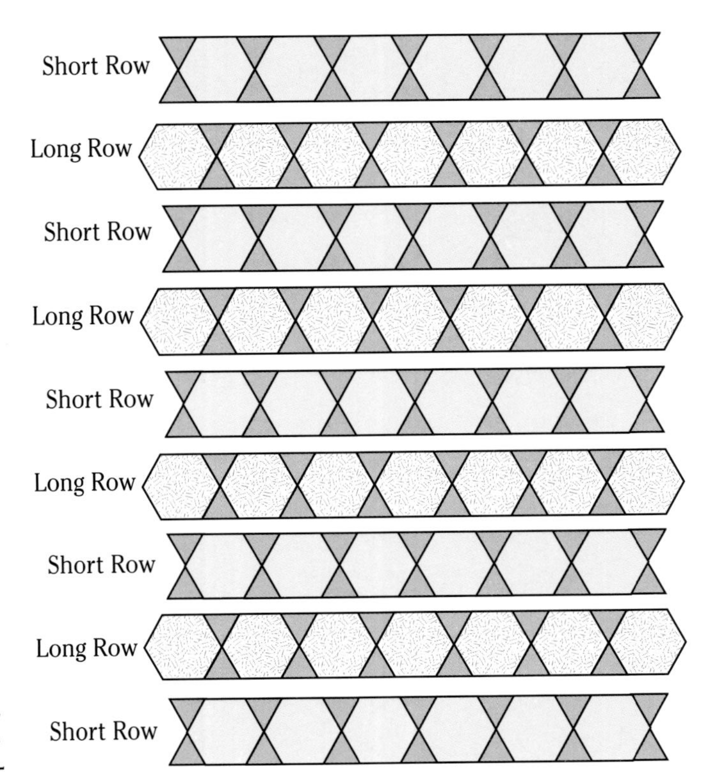

Layout of Rows

# Tree Skirt

*pieced by Donna M.J. Kinsey*
*quilted by Osie Lebowitz*

*Celebrate the season of joy. Your favorite holiday motifs dance around a tree skirt in fabrics that complement Christmas decor.*

SIZE: 37" diameter

YARDAGE:
We used *Moda* "Marble Dots" by Basics
OR use the fabric colors of your choice.
1/2 yard Red dot for wedges
1/2 yard White dot for wedges & appliques
5/8 yard Green swirl for appliques and bias binding

| | |
|---|---|
| Backing | 1 1/6 yards |
| Batting | 41" x 41" |

*Steam-a-Seam 2* fusible web for appliques
Assorted Red and White buttons for berries and tree
*DMC* Red embroidery floss, chenille needle
Sewing machine, needle, thread
*AccuQuilt® GO! baby*™ Fabric Cutter (#55300),
GO! die #55043 Holiday Medley
GO! die #55037 Baby, Baby

MAKING THE SKIRT:
Using the pattern, cut 4 Red wedges and 4 White wedges.
With right sides together, sew the sections together, alternating the colors.
Leave 1 seam open. Press.

APPLIQUES:
Apply fusible web to the wrong side of applique fabrics before cutting.
Using GO! die #55043 Holiday Medley:
Cut 2 White dot snowflakes, 6 Green leaves, 2 Green trees.
Using GO! die #55037 Baby, Baby:
Cut 2 White dot polar bears, 2 Green bowtie, 4 Green eyes.

Note: Use the wrong side of the White dot fabric to cut out the eyebrows, ear liners, and paw pads for the bear.

Fuse appliques in place.
Applique as desired.
Embroider the mouth on each bear with Red floss.

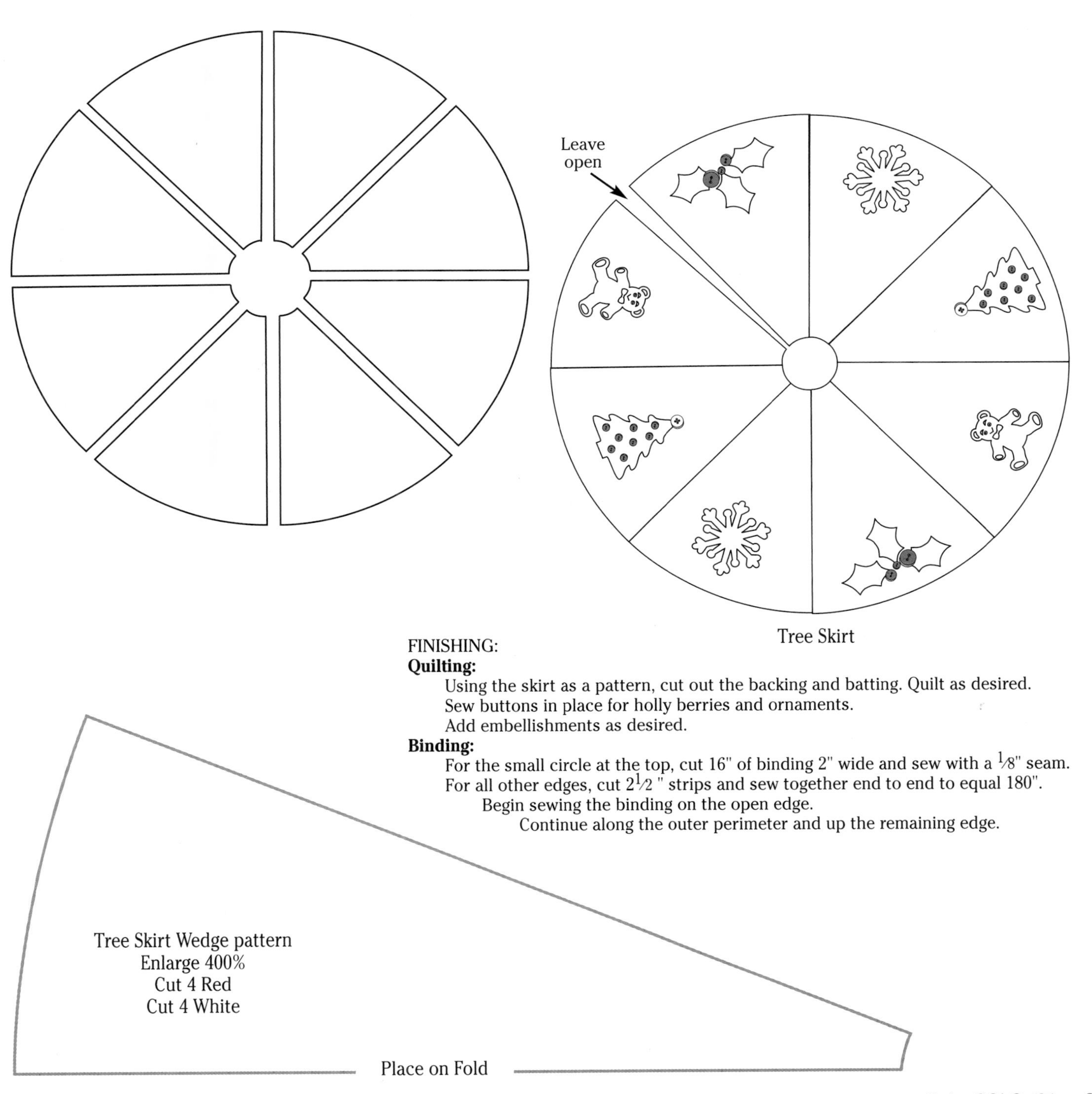


FINISHING:

**Quilting:**

Using the skirt as a pattern, cut out the backing and batting. Quilt as desired.
Sew buttons in place for holly berries and ornaments.
Add embellishments as desired.

**Binding:**

For the small circle at the top, cut 16" of binding 2" wide and sew with a 1/8" seam.
For all other edges, cut 2 1/2 " strips and sew together end to end to equal 180".
Begin sewing the binding on the open edge.
Continue along the outer perimeter and up the remaining edge.

# Easy Elegance

*pieced by Edna Summers*
*quilted by Sue Needle*

*Pretty pastels capture the elegance of times past on a quilt that is assembled with a speed and ease that would amaze your grandmother.*

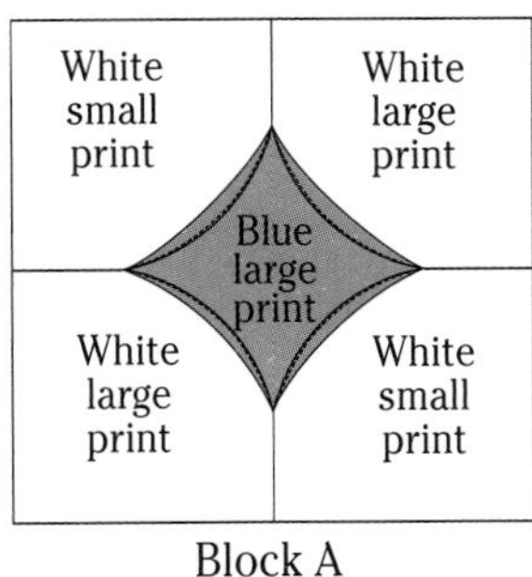


Block A
Make 6

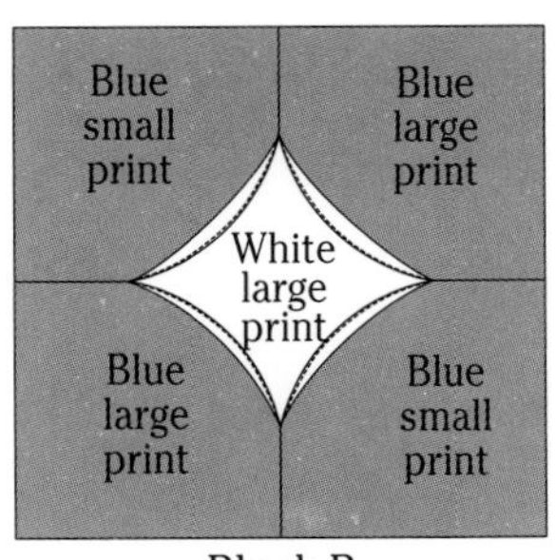


Block B
Make 6

SIZE: 37" x 46"

YARDAGE:

We used *Moda* "Charlevoix" by Polly Minick & Lauri Simpson OR use the fabric colors of your choice.

| | |
|---|---|
| Squares | 1/2 yard of Blue large print |
| Squares | 1/3 yard of White small print |
| Squares & Border #1 | 1/2 yard Blue small print |
| Squares, Border #2 & Binding | 1 1/3 yards White large print |
| Backing | 1 2/3 yards |
| Batting | 45" x 54" |

Sewing machine, needle, thread

CUTTING:

Use GO die #55010 Square 5" to die-cut the following pieces:

18 White large print squares
12 White small print squares
18 Blue large print squares
12 Blue small print squares

MAKING THE BLOCKS:

Refer to the 10-Minute Block Method - pages 30 - 31.

**Block A** -
Refer to diagram for placement of fabrics.
Make 6 of Block A.

**Block B** -
Refer to diagram for placement of fabrics.
Make 6 of Block B.

Roll back the bias edge of each center square (page 31) to make a curved edge.
Topstitch in place.

ASSEMBLY:

Arrange 4 rows of 3 blocks each on a work surface.
Sew the rows together. Press.

**Border #1:**

Cut 2 strips 1 1/2"x 36 1/2" for sides.
Cut 2 strips 1 1/2" x 29 1/2" for top and bottom.
Sew side borders to the quilt. Press.
Sew top and bottom borders to the quilt. Press.

**Border #2:**

Cut 2 strips 4 1/2"x 38 1/2" for sides.
Cut 2 strips 4 1/2" x 37 1/2" for top and bottom.
Sew side borders to the quilt. Press.
Sew top and bottom borders to the quilt. Press.

Easy Elegance - Quilt Assembly diagram

FINISHING:

**Quilt and Bind the edges:**

Sew 2 1/2" strips together end to end to equal 176".

continued on pages 30 - 31

continued from pages 28 - 29

# Basic Instructions for '10-Minute' Blocks

MAKING THE BLOCKS:
1. For each block, choose
   4 corner squares and 1 center square.
   Refer to the Block Construction diagrams.
2. Fold a square 'C' in half, wrong sides together.
3. Align the raw edges of the folded square 'C'
   with the bottom and left edges of the upper
   right corner square.

Follow the steps 4 - 14 to
complete the block.
Repeat for more blocks.
Each block (5" x 5" squares)
will measure $9\frac{1}{2}$" x $9\frac{1}{2}$" at
this point.

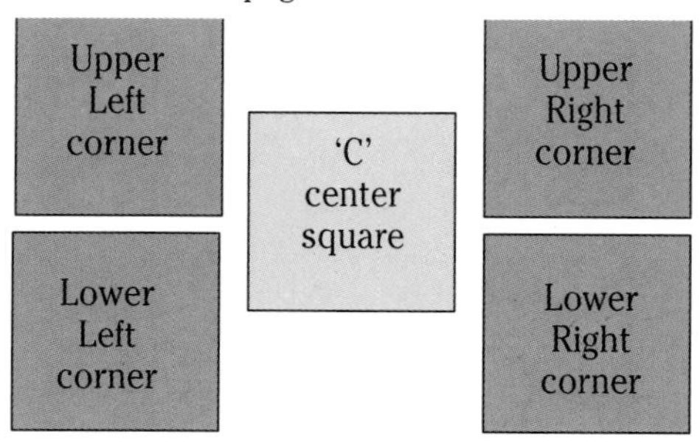


1. For each block you will need 4 corner squares and 1 'C' center square.

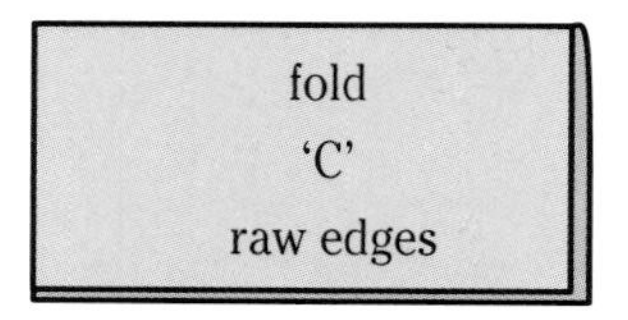


2. Fold the 'C' center square in half. with wrong sides together.

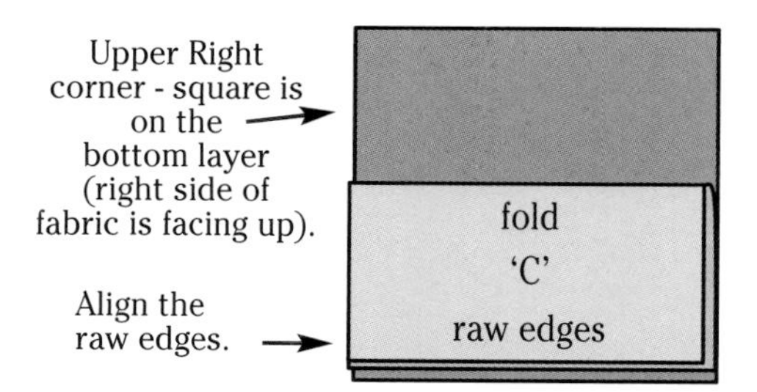


3. Align the raw edges of the 'C' folded square with the bottom and left edges of the Upper Right corner square.

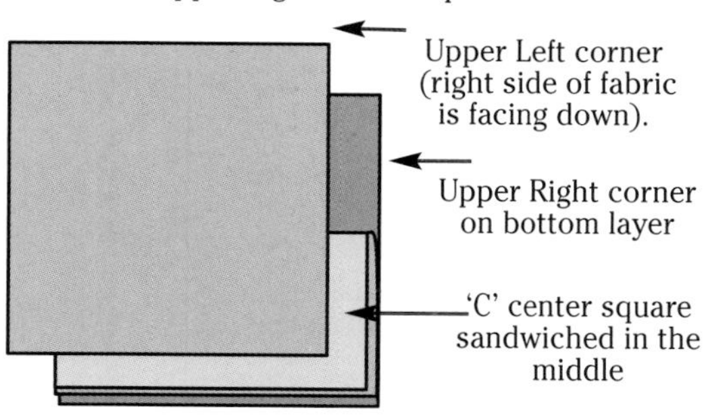


4. Sandwich the 'C' folded square between the right sides of 2 corner squares so the right sides are touching 'C'.
There should be 4 layers of fabric along the bottom.

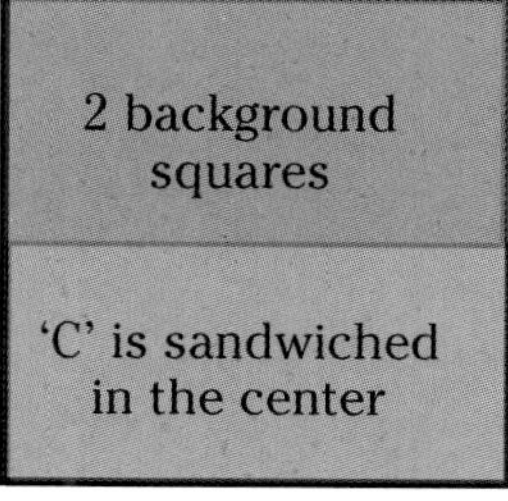


5. Align the 4 layers of fabric along the bottom.

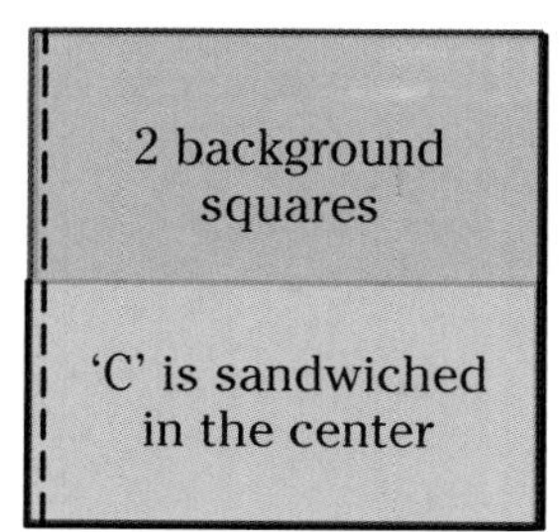


6. Sew a $\frac{1}{4}$" seam on the left-hand side.

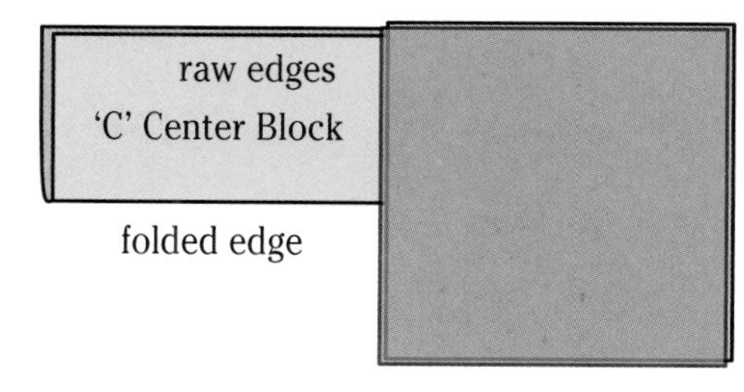


7. Open the layers so the Corner squares
meet with wrong sides together.
Turn the piece to match the diagram.

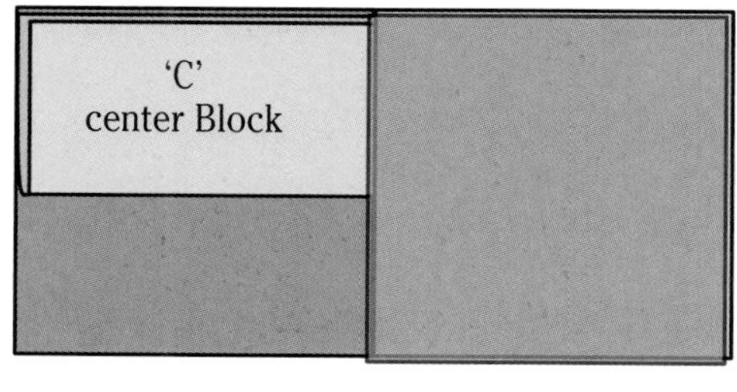


8. Place the Lower Right corner square
under 'C' folded square
(right side of fabric facing up).
Align the top and left raw edges.

9. Place the Lower Left corner square on top
(right side of fabric facing down).
This layers the 'C' folded square between the
right sides of the corner squares.
Align the left and top edges.
Sew a $\frac{1}{4}$" seam on the left side.

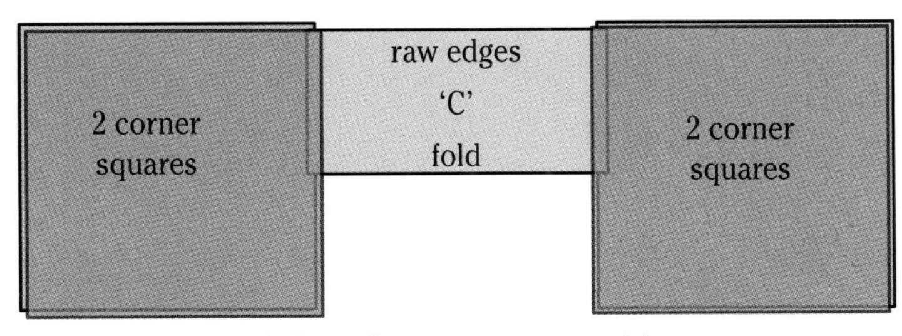


10. Open the corner squares with wrong sides together. Press.

11. Pull the 'C' center square apart.

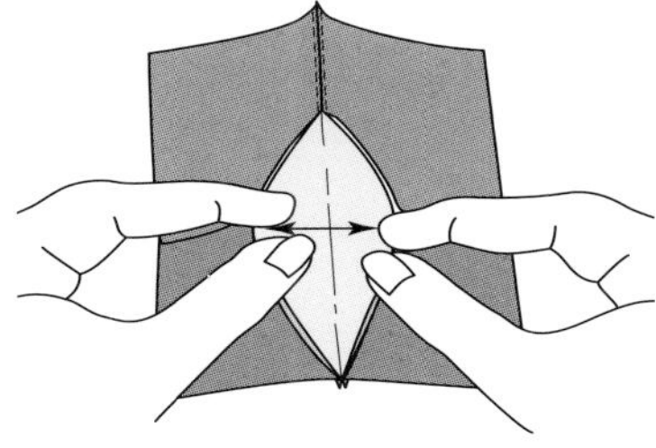

12. Flatten the seams with right sides together. (opening up the 'C' center square so it makes a diamond)

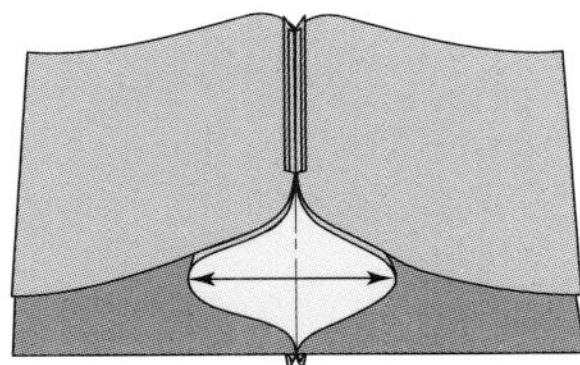

13. Pull the center shape until the shape is flat. Press

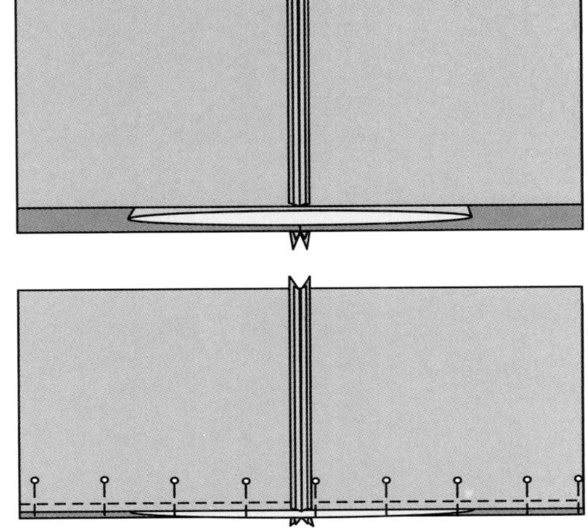

14. Pin the raw edges together making sure to line up the seams in the center.
15. Sew a $^{1}/_{4}$" seam along the bottom edge.

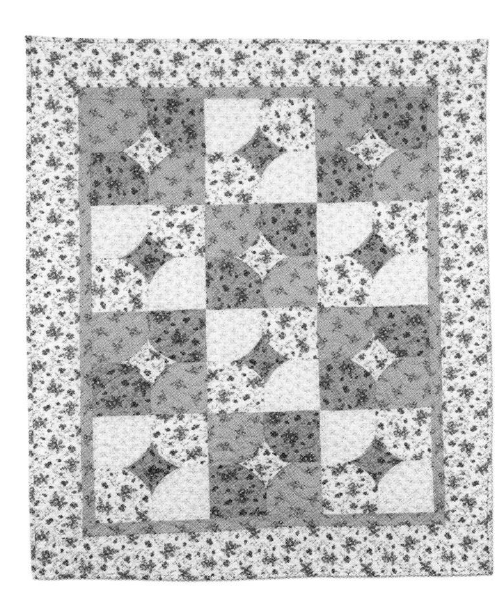

16. Open the piece and pull the center shape until it is flat and the 'C' center forms a layered diamond. Press.

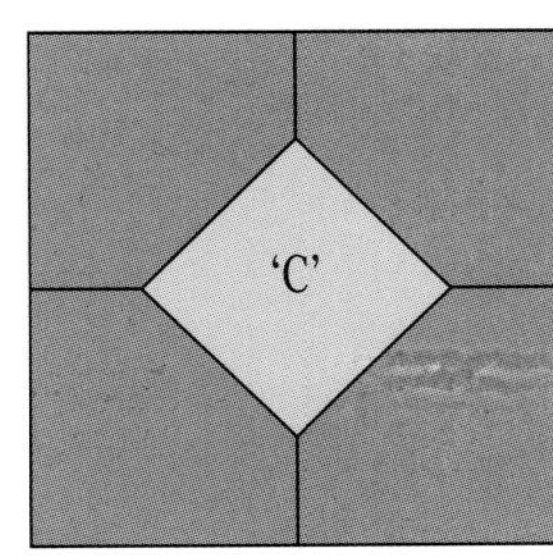


## *Cathedral Window*

*Create interesting curves in the center of each large block. This technique is simple and creates a wonderfully mysterious look.*

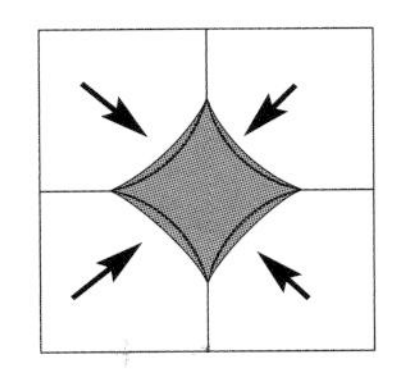

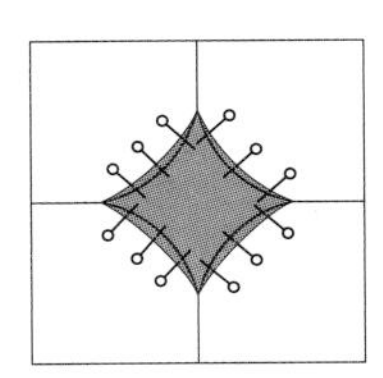

Gently pull the loose edge of each side of the center square toward the center of the block forming a curve.

Pin in place. Topstitch along the INSIDE edges of each center block to hold the edges down flat.

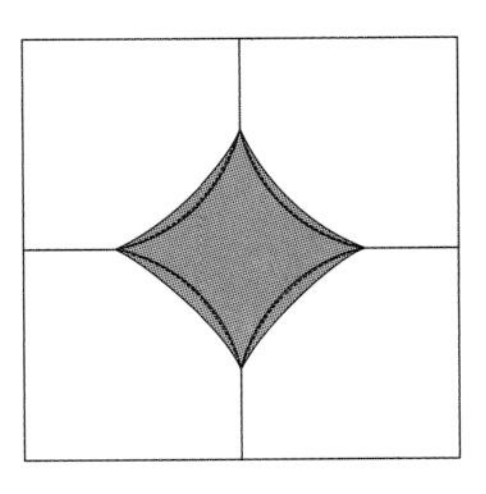

Curved Blocks in the Center

# Spring Fling Tote

*pieced by Lanelle Herron*

*Proclaim your love of sewing and fabric by making a personalized and cheerful bag guaranteed to get attention.*

*Perfect for toting your goods from the quilt show, craft fair, or grocery store, this sturdy carry-all is drenched in the sunkissed colors of spring and promises to be a year-round favorite.*

SIZE: 19" x 24"

YARDAGE:

We used *Moda* "Sunkissed" by Sweetwater
OR use the fabric colors of your choice.
5/8 yard of Gold prints - assorted check, stripe, text
1 1/3 yards of Green prints - assorted dots, check, stripe, text
1/2 yard of Green dot - for handle and border
1/2 yard of Pink - assorted check, stripe, floral, text

| | |
|---|---|
| Lining & Backing | 3/4 yard |
| Batting | 36" x 44" |

*Steam-a-Seam 2* fusible web for appliques
Sewing machine, needle, thread

*AccuQuilt® GO! baby™* Fabric Cutter (#55300),

GO! die #55030 Critters - butterfly
GO! die #55065 Calico Cat
GO! die #55064 Gingham Dog
GO! die #55007 Round Flower - petals, centers
GO! die #55042 Funky Flower
GO! die #55328 Tulip
GO! die #55334 Fun Flower
GO! die #55014 Strip Cutter 2½"

PREPARATION FOR BLOCKS:

Green - Cut an assortment of 24 strips, each 2½" x 8½".
Gold - Cut an assortment of 24 strips, each 2½" x 8½".

PREPARATION FOR HANDLES & BORDER:

Cut 4 Green dot strips, each 2½" x 36".
Cut 4 Green dot strips for the border 3½" x 24½".
Cut 2 batting strips, each 2½" x 36".

PREPARATION FOR LINING:

Cut 2 lining pieces, each 16½" x 24½".

PREPARATION FOR QUILT BACKING:

Cut 2 backing pieces, each 20½" x 26½".
Cut 2 batting pieces, each 20½" x 26½".

PREPARATION FOR APPLIQUES:

Apply fusible web to the back of fabrics before cutting.
Die cut all pieces as listed below:

| **Color** | #55030 Butterfly, #55065 Cat, #55064 Dog |
|---|---|
| assorted Pink | 1 wing, 1 body<br>2 cats, 1 in reverse, 1 dog, 1 ear |
| **Color** | #55007 Round Flower, #55042 Funky Flower |
| assorted Pink | 1 large flower, 2 hexagon centers, 3 small circles, 1 large circle, 1 flower center, 1 large flower |
| **Color** | #55328 Tulip, #55334 Fun Flower |
| assorted Pink | 5 tulip centers, 1 large flower |

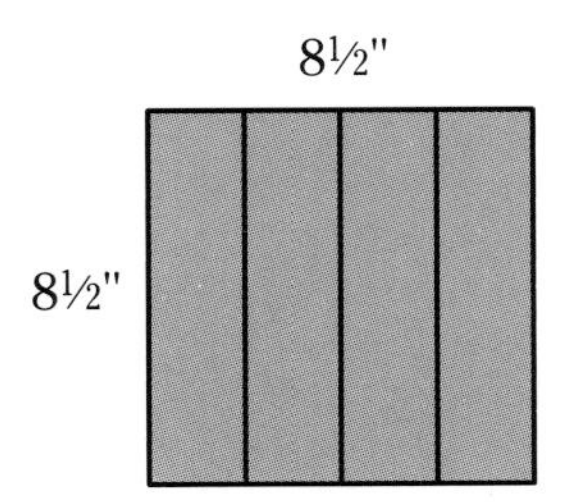

Green Blocks - Make 6

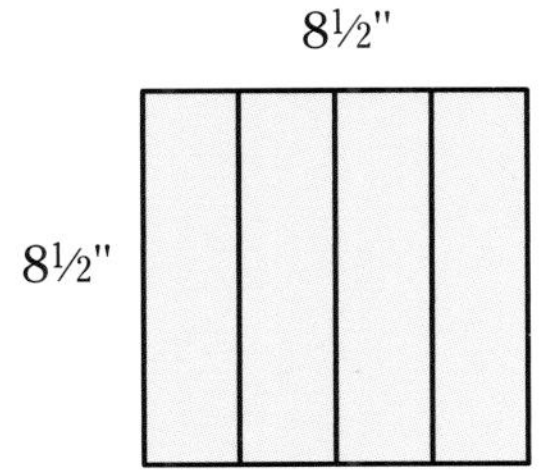

Gold Blocks - Make 6

MAKE THE BLOCKS:

Make 6 Green blocks (3 each for front and back).
Make 6 Gold blocks (3 each for front and back).
For each block, choose 4 strips.
Sew 4 strips together to make a square 8½" x 8½".
Press.

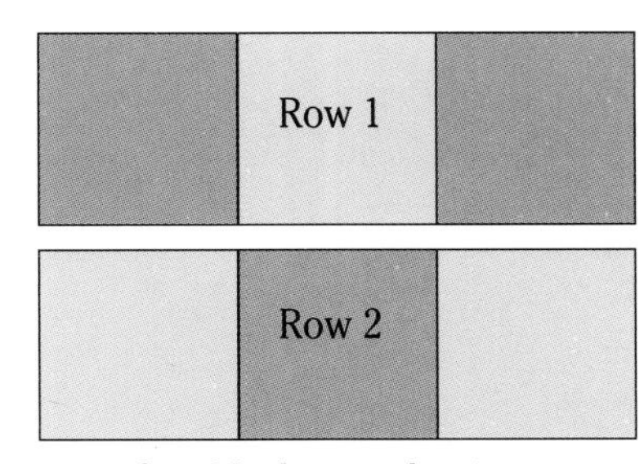

Sew blocks together in rows.
Make 2 of each row.

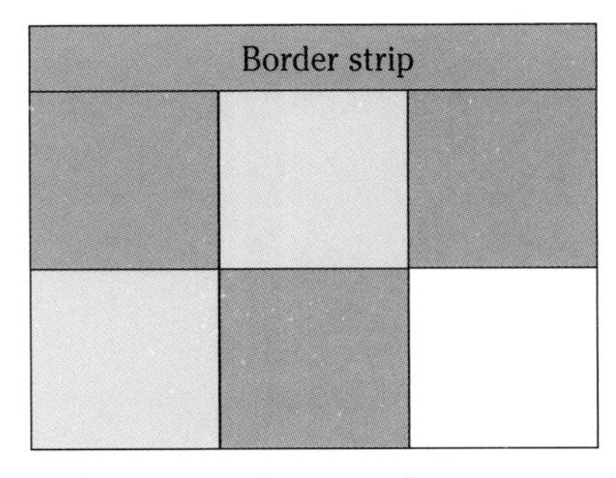

Sew 2 rows together to make a tote panel.
Sew a border strip to the top of the front of the tote.
Sew a border strip to the top of the back of the tote.

APPLIQUE:

Position the pieces as follows:

**Green Block 1:**
Layer the Pink Tulip, Fun flower, Hexagon center, and a Circle.
Fuse in place.

**Gold Block 2:** Fuse Pink Cats in place.

**Green Block 3:**
Layer a Pink Funky flower, a Floral center, and a Small circle.
Fuse in place.

**Gold Block 4:**
Fuse butterfly wings and body in place.

**Green Block 5:**
Layer a Pink Flower, a Hexagon, a Large circle, and a Small circle.
Fuse in place.

**Gold Block 6:**
Fuse dog and ear in place.
Applique as desired.

QUILTING:

Layer a backing, batting and the front panel of the tote.
Echo quilt around the appliques.
Topstitch in the ditch through all 3 layers.

Repeat for the back of the tote.

continued on page 34

continued from page 33

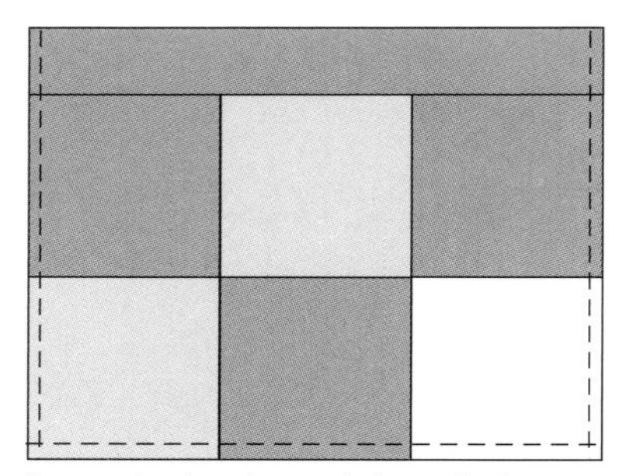

Sew up both sides and along the bottom.

ASSEMBLY:

**Sew the Front to the Back:**

Position the front side and back side with right sides together.
Sew the front to the back at the sides and along the bottom.

**Make the Lining:**

Sew a border strip to the top of each lining piece. Press.
With right sides together, sew the lining front to the back along the sides and bottom.
Leave an 8" opening in one side for turning.
Turn the lining right side out.

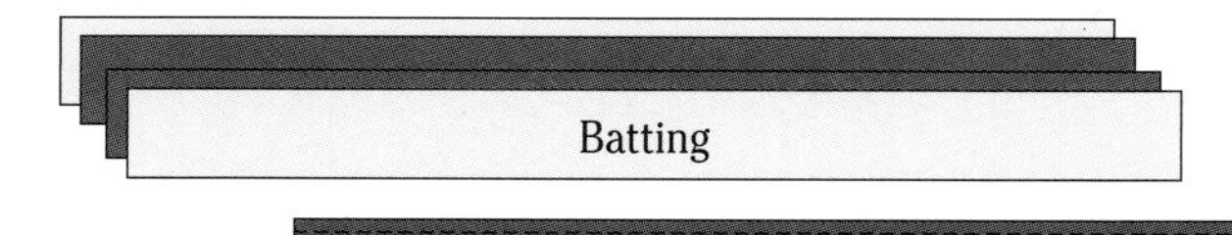


**Handles:**

Place 2 strips right sides together.
Place 1 strip of batting on top and place 1 strip underneath.

Sew both long sides to make a tube.
Turn right sides out. Press.
Topstitch 1/2" away from each edge.

Repeat for the second handle.
Pin the handles in place on the outside of tote.

**Lining the Tote:**

Place the lining inside of the tote so right sides are together.
Sew a 1/4" seam around the top edge.

Turn the tote right side out by pulling the quilted side through the opening in the lining.
Push the lining snugly into the tote.

Hand stitch the opening in the lining closed.
Topstitch 1/4" from the top around the tote being sure to topstitch several times over the end of each handle through all layers.

continued from page 25

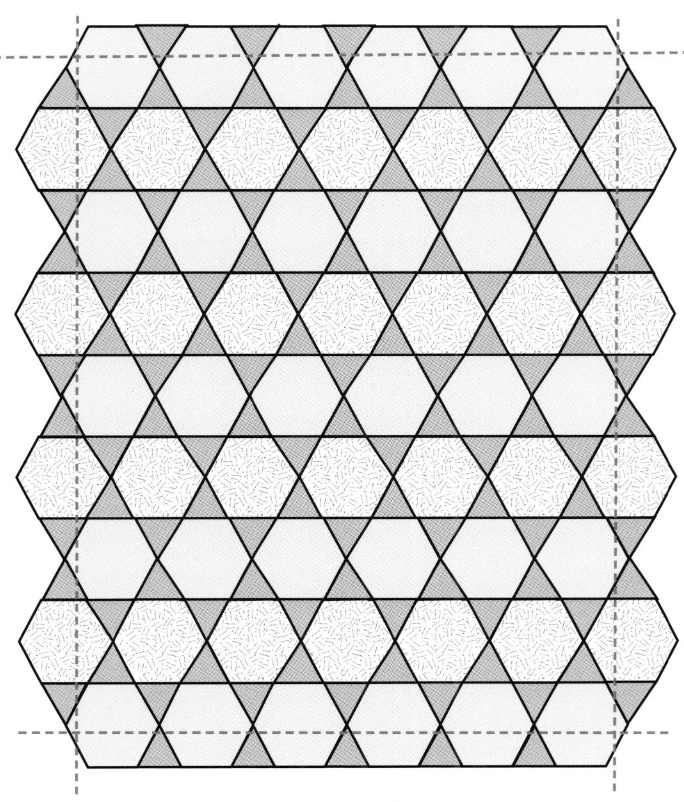

Diagram 5-A
Trim the Side Rows. Trim the Top & Bottom Rows

Hexagon Quilt Assembly Diagram

Finished Quilt

ASSEMBLY:

Sew the rows together. Press.

Center the quilt and carefully trim the sides 1/4" outside the point of the Blue triangles (width 26" x height 30 1/2").

**Border #1 -**

Cut the border print into strips 5 1/2" wide.

Cut 2 strips 30 1/2" long for sides.

Cut 2 strips 26" long for top and bottom.

Cut 4 Red print 5 1/2" squares for cornerstones.

Sew side borders to the quilt. Press.

Sew a cornerstone to each end of the top and bottom borders. Press.

Sew top and bottom borders to the quilt. Press.

FINISHING:

**Quilt and Bind the edges:**

Sew 2 1/2" strips together end to end to equal 162".

## Olivia the Octopus

*by Donna Arends Hansen*

*What's squeezably soft with plenty of arms for hugging? Why, it's your child's newest favorite toy. This cuddly creature is made entirely from scraps! It's a quick 2-hour project.*

## Rachel the Rag Doll

*by Donna Arends Hansen*

*Who can resist this friendly face and gorgeous hair? Rachel is ready to play or smile from a special spot in your daughter's room.*

see instructions on pages 38 - 39

# Olivia the Octopus

SIZE: 23" diameter x 30" long

YARDAGE:
We used a mix of 18 pastel strips, each 2½" x 42"
OR use the fabric colors of your choice.
½ yard of pastel Pink
½ yard of pastel Green
½ yard of pastel Blue
2 Blue ¾" buttons for eyes (DO NOT use buttons on toys)
Polyfil stuffing
*Steam-a-Seam 2* fusible web for appliques
Two 18" pieces of Pink ⅜" ribbon
Sewing machine, needle, thread

*AccuQuilt® GO! baby*™ Fabric Cutter (#55300),
GO! die #55014 Strip Cutter 2½"
GO! die #55008 Feather
GO! die #55029 Hearts - 2", 3" 4"

PREPARATION:
Die cut all pieces as listed below.
Cut an assortment of 18 strips, each 2½" x 42".
Cut 6 strips, each 2½" x 21" and set them aside for braid.

PREPARATION FOR APPLIQUES:
Apply fusible web to the back of fabrics before cutting.
Die cut all pieces as listed below.

| | |
|---|---|
| Eyes | 2 White straight feathers #55008 Feather |
| Mouth | 1 Red 2" Heart #55029 Hearts |

MAKE THE BODY:
Arrange 12 strips to make a piece 24½" x 42".
Starting at a point 6" from the end of the strip, sew for 12" and stop, leaving 24" for the braided arms.
Sew all 12 strips together in this manner. Press.

APPLIQUES:
Cut the points off the feathers to create the eye shape.
Find the center of the 12" sewn section.
Fuse the eyes and heart mouth in place.
Applique as desired.
Zigzag stitch a mouth across the center of the heart.
Sew the buttons to the eyes.
Caution: Do Not use buttons on toys for small children. Embroider the eyes instead.

PREPARE THE LEGS:
Now use the 2½" x 21" strips that you set aside.
Aligning the bottom edges of the strips, place a 21" strip on each of the 12 free strands to be braided

Sew the top end of each 21" strip securely in place.

Fold the body with right sides together, forming a tube.
Sew across the open edge to secure the legs.
Turn right sides out.

ASSEMBLY:
**Head** - Wrap 1 ribbon around the strips at the 6" mark.
Wrap ribbon several times and secure tightly with a knot.
Tie a bow on the outside.
Tack the ribbon in place.
Stuff the head until full and puffy with polyfil.

BRAID THE LEGS:
Separate the 24 arm strands into 8 groups of 3.
Braid each leg and tie a knot at the end.
**Legs** - Wrap ribbon around the strips at the 12" mark.
Wrap ribbon several times and secure tightly with a knot.
Tie a bow on the outside.
Tack the ribbon in place.

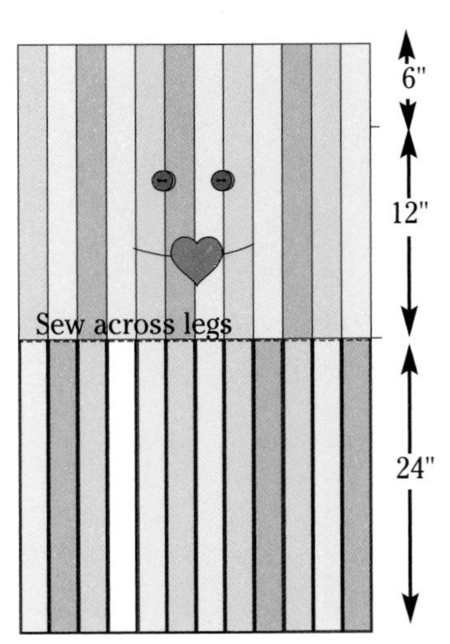

Applique Placement

## Loving Hearts Banner

SIZE: 4" wide x 72"

YARDAGE: We used 5" x 5" scraps of 9 different Red prints, 72" of $\frac{3}{8}$" ribbon
*Steam-a-Seam 2* fusible web for appliques, Sewing machine, needle, thread
*AccuQuilt® GO! baby™* Fabric Cutter (#55300), GO! die #55029 Hearts - 2", 3" 4"

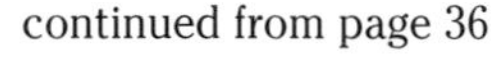

continued from page 36

## Rachel the Rag Doll

SIZE: 23" diameter x 30" long

YARDAGE:

We used *Moda* "Charlevoix" by Minick & Simpson
- $\frac{2}{3}$ yard of White ($\frac{1}{6}$ solid and $\frac{1}{2}$ print)
- $\frac{1}{2}$ yard of Gold
- $\frac{1}{2}$ yard of Yellow
- $\frac{1}{2}$ yard of Blue

24" of $\frac{1}{2}$" wide ribbon for tying the dress
2 Black $\frac{1}{2}$" buttons (DO NOT use buttons on toys)
*DMC* Black floss, chenille needle
Polyfil batting and stuffing
*Pellon* heavy weight fusible interfacing (stabilizer)
*Steam-a-Seam 2* fusible web for appliques
Sewing machine, needle, thread

*AccuQuilt® GO! baby™* Fabric Cutter (#55300),
GO! die #55014 Strip Cutter $2\frac{1}{2}$"
GO! die #55012 Circles - 2", 3", 5"

PREPARATION:

Cut all pieces as listed below.

**FACE:**

Press heavy weight interfacing to the back of fabric.

| | |
|---|---|
| Face | 2 White 5" circles |

**BODY:**

| | |
|---|---|
| Face Batting | 2 batting of each size circle (2", 3", 5") |
| Arms & Legs | 12 White $2\frac{1}{2}$" strips, each 21" long |
| Neck | 1 White $3\frac{1}{2}$" x $6\frac{1}{2}$" piece |
| Body | 2 White $6\frac{1}{2}$" x $12\frac{1}{2}$" pieces |
| Dress | 1 Blue $12\frac{1}{2}$" x $18\frac{1}{2}$" piece |
| Ruffle | 1 Blue $3\frac{1}{2}$"x $24\frac{1}{2}$" strip |
| Hair | 21 Gold/Yellow $2\frac{1}{2}$" strips, each 21" long |

Press each strip in half to make $1\frac{1}{4}$" wide strips.

MAKE THE FACE AND HEAD:

Embroider the nose and mouth on 1 White circle.
Sew buttons for eyes. Caution: Do Not use buttons on toys for small children. Embroider the eyes.
Place a White circle (back of the head) on the table.
Place a 5" batting circle on top.
Pin hair strips around the edge, in 7 groups of 3, stacking as needed.
Topstitch to secure.
Layer both 3", both 2", and a 5" batting circle on top.
Top with the White face, with the right side up.
Pin the layers together and set aside.

MAKE THE BODY:

**Neck -** Press heavy weight interfacing to the back of the neck piece. Fold twice to $1\frac{3}{4}$"x $3\frac{1}{2}$". Press folds.

**Body -** Position body pieces with right sides together, sandwiching the strips for the arms and legs.
Sew all around, leaving an opening for turning.
Turn right side out.
Stuff body with polyfil. Stitch the opening closed.

**Attach Head -** Insert neck into head and stitch securely all around the edge of the circle. Remove pins.

**Braid** the hair, arms and legs. Knot the ends.

DRESS:

Cut 2" vertical openings for the armholes.
Sew a $\frac{1}{2}$" hem on the top of dress (to form casing for ribbon).
Thread the ribbon through the casing.

RUFFLE:

Sew a $\frac{1}{8}$" hem on one long side of the ruffle.
Sew a Gathering stitch $\frac{1}{8}$" from the edge on long edge of ruffle.
Gather the ruffle and sew it onto the bottom of the dress. Sew a $\frac{1}{8}$" hem on any remaining raw edges.
Position the dress on the doll.
Thread the arms through the armholes and gather the dress at the neck with the ribbon.
Tie the ribbon in a bow.

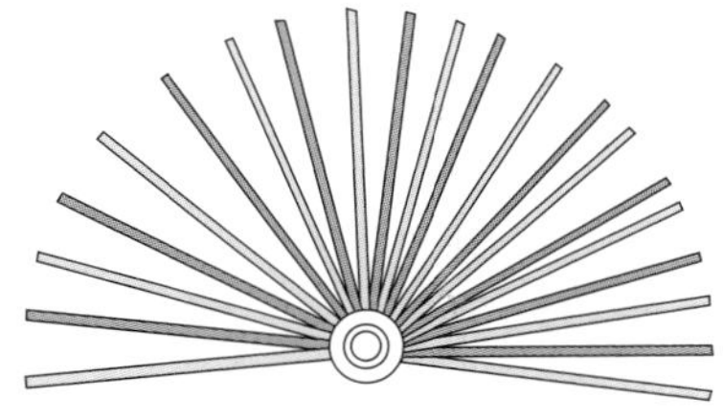

Back of Head

PREPARATION FOR BLOCKS:

Apply fusible web to the back of fabrics before cutting
Die cut six 4" hearts, four 3" hearts and eight 2" hearts. Remove the paper from fusible web.
Position half the hearts on an ironing surface with ribbon running across the hearts.
Position the center of the ribbon in the hearts.
Position the remaining hearts over their mates and fuse together, sandwiching the ribbon. Topstitch around the edges of hearts.

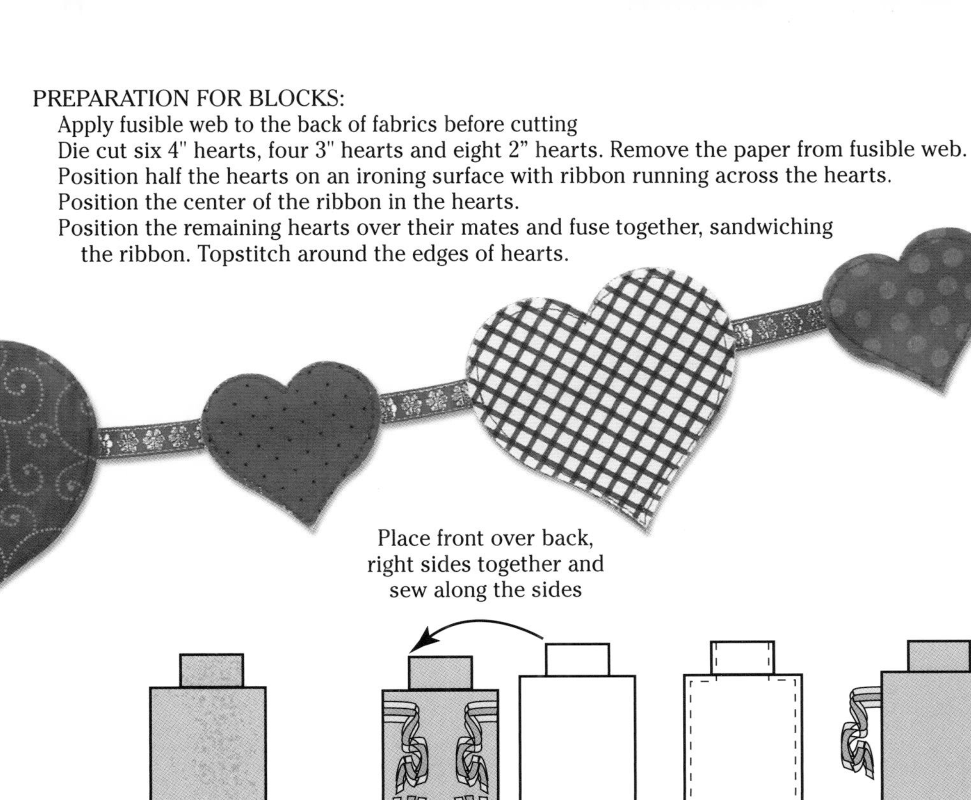

Place front over back, right sides together and sew along the sides

Body Diagram
Make 2
(1 front, 1 back)

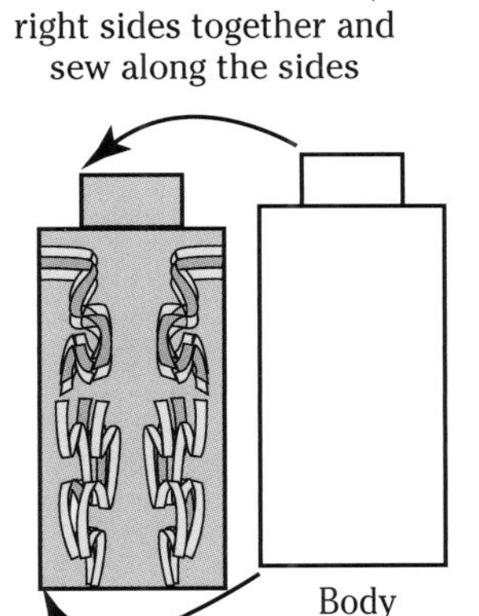

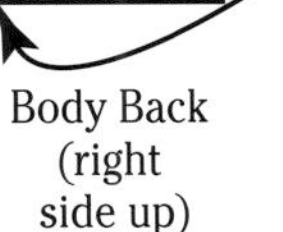

Body Back (right side up)

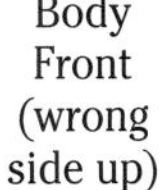

Body Front (wrong side up)

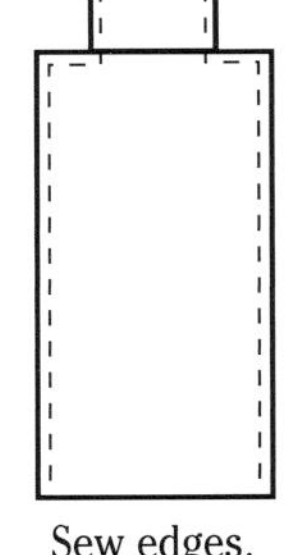

Sew edges. Turn right side out

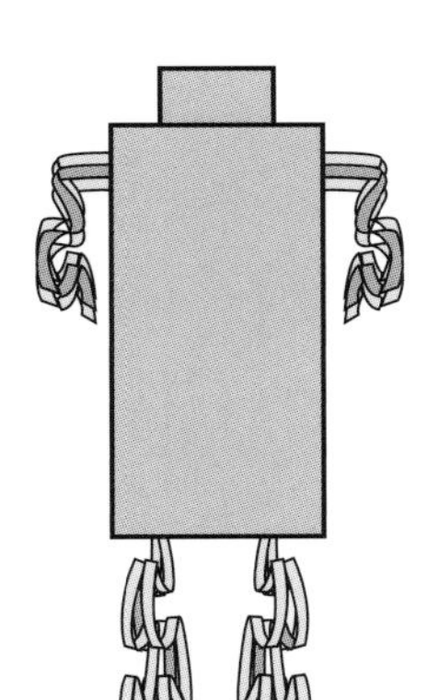

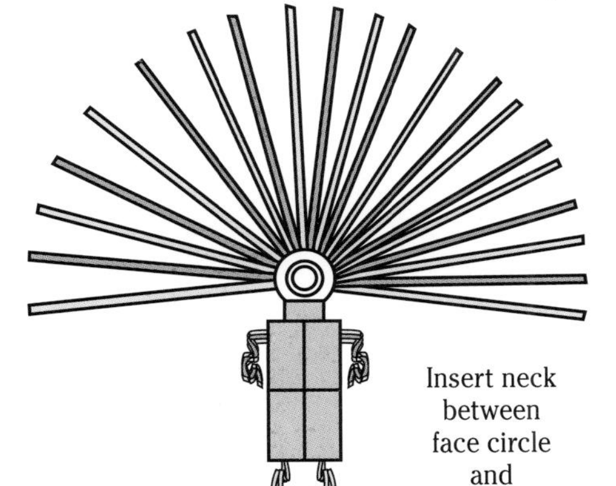

Insert neck between face circle and head circle

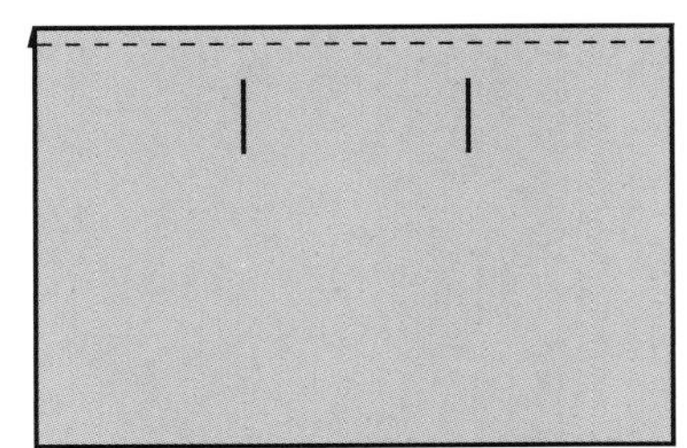

Dress with slits for arms

Ruffle

# Rag Braided Toys

*by Donna Arends Hansen*

*From scraps to toys! "Hug them, love them, wear them out. Don't worry, if you wear it out, I'll make you a new one." This promise is easy to keep because these quick and easy rag toys are a joy to sew and stitch up in no time.*

SIZE: Octopus 5" x 15", Girl 6" x 20"
YARDAGE:
We used *Moda* "Fresh" for the Octopus OR use the fabric colors of your choice.
- 1 yard of Green prints for octopus arms
- 5" x 10" of Blue print for octopus face/head
- 5" x 5" of White print for octopus eyes
- 1/2 yard of White prints for arms & legs
- 1/2 yard of Red prints for hair, body and dress
- 7" x 10" of White solid for girl's face/head/neck

*DMC* floss (Black, Red), chenille needle

10" of 1/4" wide elastic
Poly-fil stuffing
*Steam-a-Seam 2* fusible web for appliques
*Pellon* heavy weight fusible interfacing (stabilizer)
Sewing machine, needle, thread

*AccuQuilt® GO! baby*™ Fabric Cutter (#55300),
- GO! die #55014 Strip Cutter 2 1/2"
- GO! die #55012 Circles - 2", 3", 5"
- GO! die #55061 Sunbonnet Sue

PREPARATION:
Die cut all pieces as listed below.

**Hair, Arms, Legs -**

| | |
|---|---|
| Octopus | 24 Green strips, each 21" long |
| Hair | 18 Red strips, each 9" long |
| Arms & Legs | 18 White strips, each 14" long |

Press each strip in half to make 1 1/4" wide strips.

HEADS:
Press heavy weight interfacing to the back of fabric.

| | |
|---|---|
| Octopus Head | 2 Blue 5" circles |
| Girl's Head | 2 White 5" circles |

DESIGN THE FACES:
Apply fusible web to applique fabrics.
**Octopus -** Die cut 2 White arms using Sue die. Applique to octopus Blue face for eyes. Embroider a Red mouth.
**Girl -** Embroider nose and mouth on girl's face. Use buttons or embroider the eyes.

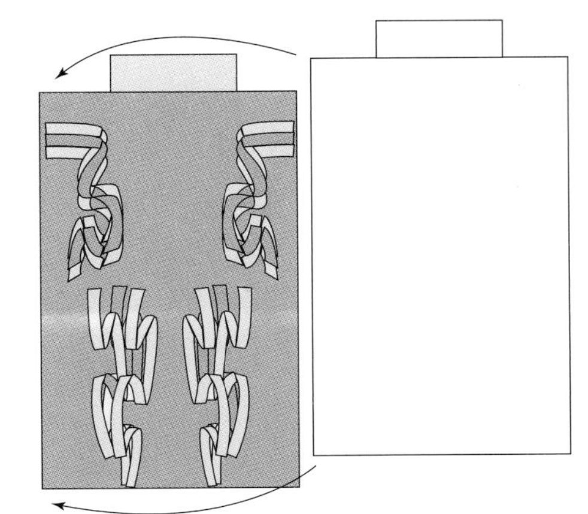

Doll Body Detail
Baste arms and legs to right side of back. Place front right side down on back and sew along sides and bottom, e neck open for stuffing.

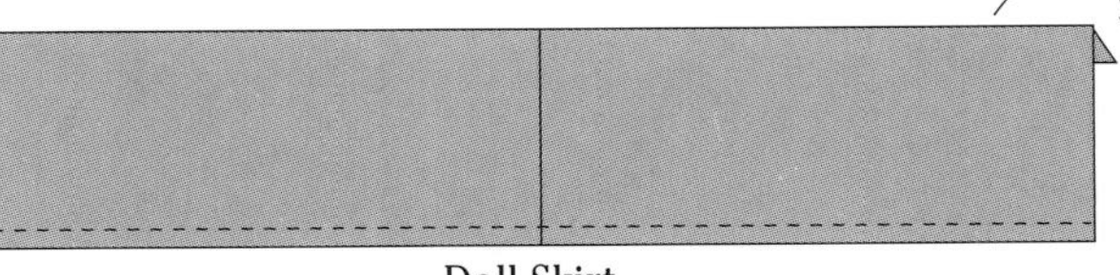

Doll Skirt

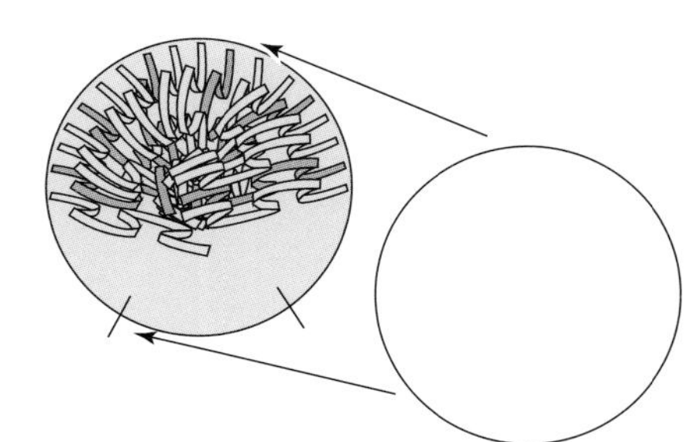

Doll Head Detail
Baste hair to right side of head back. Place head front right side down on back and sew leaving opening for stuffing.

Octopus Face Detail

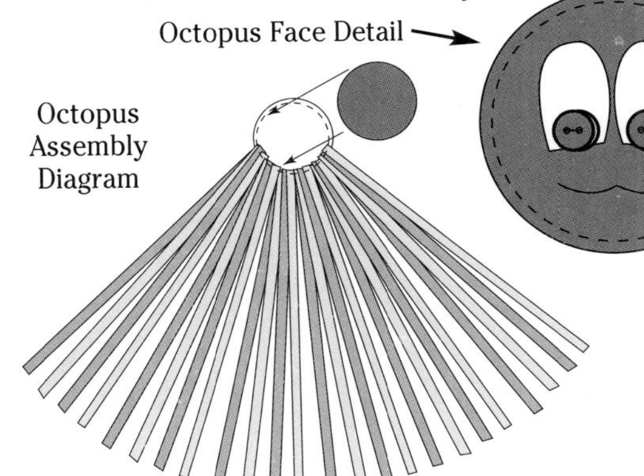

Octopus Assembly Diagram

MAKE THE OCTOPUS:
Place a Blue circle on the table wrong side up. Pin the arm strips in 8 groups of 3 on the bottom edge, stacking as needed. Topstitch to secure.
Place the other Blue circle on top. Topstitch around the edge of the circle, leaving an opening for stuffing.
Stuff and sew the opening closed.
Braid the legs. Tie a knot on the end.

MAKE THE GIRL'S BODY:
**Neck -** Cut 1 White 3 1/2" x 6 1/2" piece. Press heavy weight interfacing to the back. Fold twice to 1 3/4"x 3 1/2". Press folds.
**Body -** Cut 2 Red pieces, each 3 1/2" x 8 1/2".
Sew body pieces together, sandwiching the arms, legs and neck. Sew all around, leaving an opening for turning. Turn right side out. Stuff body with polyfil. Stitch the opening closed. Braid the arms and legs. Knot the ends.

MAKE THE SKIRT:
Cut 1 Red skirt, 3 1/2" x 18 1/2".
Sew a 1/8" hem along 1 long side. This will be the bottom of the skirt.
Sew a 1/2" hem along the top to make the elastic casing.
Thread elastic into the casing and stitch the ends in place.
With right sides together, sew the short ends to make a tube. Turn right side out. Slide the skirt onto the doll.

MAKE THE GIRL'S HEAD:
Place the back of the head on the table right side up and position the hair in 6 groups of 3 around the top of head.
Baste hair in place.
Place the face on top, face down.
Sew around the edge of the circle leaving an opening for stuffing. Turn right side out. Stuff. Sew the opening closed.
Securely sew neck to back of head.
Braid the hair and knot the ends.

SIZE: 5" x 8"

YARDAGE:

We used *Moda* “Full Circle” by Kathy Schmitz OR use the fabric colors of your choice.

1 Fat quarter each of Tan, Burgundy and Black
2 buttons (Do Not use buttons on articles for children)
*Steam-a-Seam 2* fusible web for appliques
*Pellon* heavy weight fusible interfacing (stabilizer)
Sewing machine, needle, thread

*AccuQuilt® GO! baby*™ Fabric Cutter (#55300),
GO! die #55012 Circles - 2", 3", 5"
GO! die #55029 Hearts - 2", 3", 5"
GO! die #55061 Sunbonnet Sue

Ear Pattern Cut 2 of each

PREPARATION FOR PURSE:

To stiffen fabrics, fuse interfacing to the back before cutting.
Die cut all pieces as listed below.

| | |
|---|---|
| **Face & Purse Backs** | 4 Burgundy 5" circles |
| **Ears** | 2 Burgundy 3" circles |
| | 2 Black circles 3" for back of ears |
| **Flower** | 2 Black 2" circles |

PREPARATION FOR APPLIQUES:

Apply fusible web to the back of applique fabrics before cutting.
Die cut all pieces as listed below .

| | |
|---|---|
| **Inner Ears & Mouth** | 2 Tan 2" circles, 1 Tan 5" circle |
| **Mouth** | 1 Burgundy 2" heart |
| **Eyes** | 2 Tan arms |

ASSEMBLE THE FACE:

**Ears -** Fuse 2" Tan circles to the Burgundy ear fronts.
**Mouth -** Cut a 2" strip out of the center of 1 Tan 5" circle.
**Face -** Fuse eyes, mouth pieces and heart in place.
Applique as desired. Sew buttons or embroider the eyes.

PURSE ASSEMBLY:

Match 2 Burgundy purse backs. Sew together on the edge.
Sandwich ears between Face and purse back. Pin securely.
Sew together on the edge.

**Front & Back -** Match purse front and purse back. Leaving the top of the purse open, sew around the edge from the top of one ear to the top of the other ear.

**Strip -** Cut a Black strap 2½" x 30". Fold strap in half lengthwise, with right sides together. Sew the long end. Turn right side out. Attach strap to the front next to each ear.

# Monkey Purse

*by Donna Arends Hansen*

*Don't monkey around trying to find your cell phone or wallet. This whimsical purse is just the right size to keep necessary items at hand.*

Mouth Cut 2

Monkey Assembly

**Flower -** Sew 2 Black circles together. Fold into a flower shape and sew to the purse over the end of strap.

# Holiday Ornaments

*by Donna Arends Hansen*

SIZE: tree 4" wide x 5½" tall
holly berry 4" wide x 4" tall

YARDAGE:
10" x 10" each of 3 Green print fabrics
Assorted buttons
20" of ribbon for each ornament hanger
*Steam-a-Seam 2* fusible web
Hot glue gun, hot glue

*AccuQuilt® GO! baby™* Fabric Cutter (#55300),
GO! die #55043 Holiday Medley
GO! die #55012 Circles - 2", 3", 5"

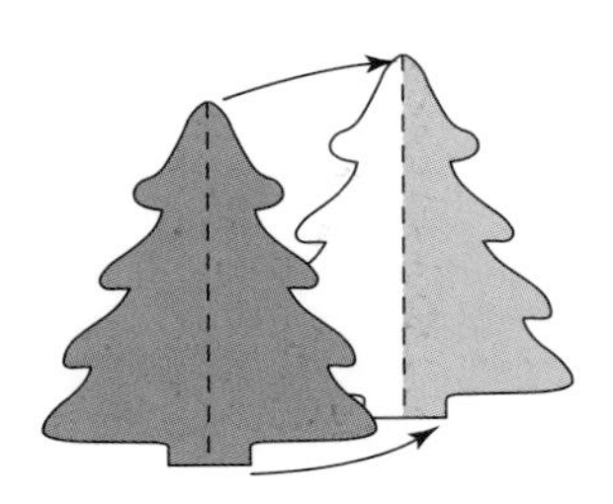

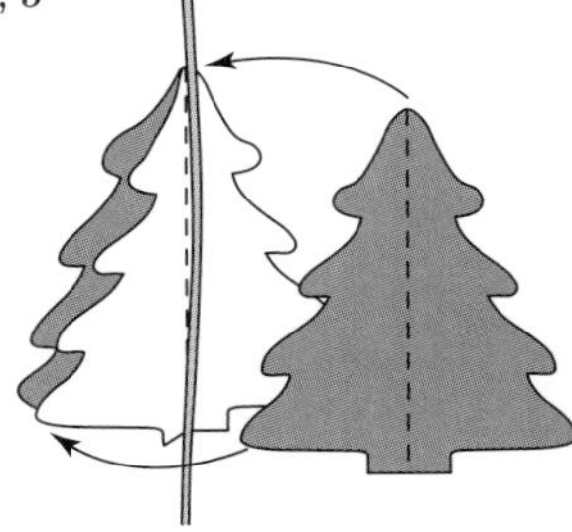

## Tree Ornament

Apply fusible web to fabrics before cutting. Die cut 3 trees.
Fold and press 2 trees from the tip through the trunk.
Set 1 tree aside.
On 2 trees, remove paper backing on one side of the fold line so half of each tree can be fused together back to back.
Fuse together. Remove all paper backing.
Lay a folded ribbon loop along the fold line, leaving a tail at the bottom for threading the buttons.
Fuse the 3rd tree in place, sandwiching the ribbon.
Decorate with buttons.

## Holly Berry Ornament

Apply fusible web to Green fabrics before cutting.
Die cut 4 holly leaves (2 in reverse).
Fuse 2 leaves together back to back. Make 2.
Die cut 1 Red 3" circle. Make a Yo-Yo.
Sew holly leaves and buttons to the Yo-Yo.

## How to Make a Yo-Yo

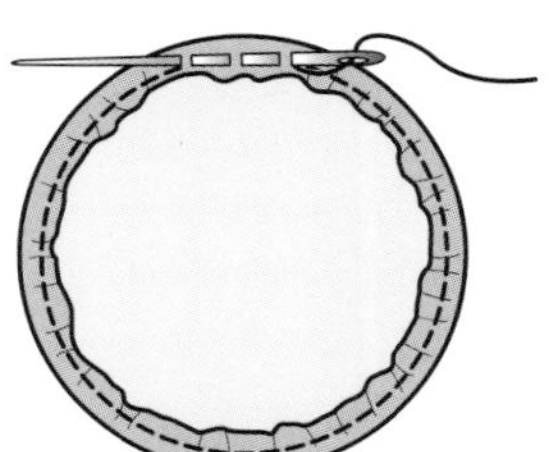

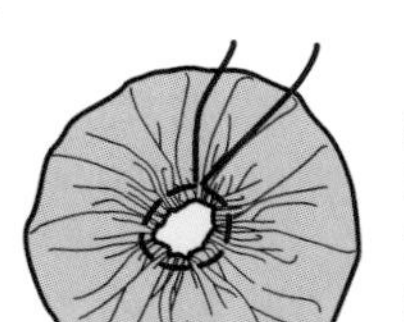

Step 2.
Pull the ends of the thread to form gathers. Tuck the fabric edges under then tie ends of thread together.

Step 1. Cut a 3" circle from fabric. Press under ¼" on the edge.
With a needle and thread, use a large Running stitch on folded edge.

# Perky Pincushions

*by Donna Arends Hansen*

*Keep your pins and needles accessible with pincushions made from scraps. Pretty colors and perky attitudes express your creativity and individual taste.*

*The wrist band is particularly helpful when you take your hand sewing out on the porch, in the car, or to your guild meeting. Brighten your day with a potted pincushion or stuffed ladybug... just for fun.*

YARDAGE AND SUPPLIES:
- We used fabric scraps
- Assorted buttons
- Poly-fil stuffing
- Pinking shears
- Chenille needle
- 2 Velcro dots for Wrist Cushion closure, Small flower pots
- Light gauge wire, Wire cutters, Needle-nose pliers
- *Steam-a-Seam 2* fusible web for fusing flower pieces together
- Sewing machine, needle, thread

*AccuQuilt® GO! baby™* Fabric Cutter (#55300),
- GO! die #55012 Circles - 2", 3", 5"
- GO! die #55007 Round Flower - petals, centers
- GO! die #55042 Funky Flower
- GO! die #55014 Strip Cutter 2½"
- GO! die #55334 Fun Flower

Press Cushion into Pot

# PINCUSHIONS IN POTS

**Flower Pot Flower Cushion**

Die cut one 5" circle.
Die cut 2 flowers.

**Pottery Cup Flowers Cushion**

Die cut one 5" circle.
Die cut 6 small flowers.

ASSEMBLY:

Gather the edge of circle with strong thread.
Fill it with stuffing, pull the gather and tie a knot.
Put a handful of pebbles or stones in the bottom as a weight to keep the pot from being knocked over easily.
Push cushion into the pot securely. Glue cushion in place.

WIRED FLOWERS:

Apply fusible web to the back of fabric.
Die cut the flower shapes (see above).
Place a flower (fusible web up) on an ironing surface.
Cut wires to 6" in length. Use pliers to curl both ends of wire.
Place a wire on each petal.
Cover with another flower and fuse together.
Pin flowers to the cushion or sew the flower center to the pincushion with a button.

Assembly Diagram

# WRIST PINCUSHION

**Wrist Flower Cushion**

Die cut one 3" circle.
Die cut 4 large flowers (2 of each shape)
Die cut a $2\frac{1}{2}$" x $9\frac{1}{2}$" side panel strip.

WIRED FLOWERS:

Follow the instructions above.

ASSEMBLY:

Gather the edge of circle with strong thread.
Fill it with stuffing, pull the gather tight and tie a knot.
Sew strip into a strap and attach Velcro dots.
Assemble with strong thread by going through a button, the cushion, both flowers and the strap several times.

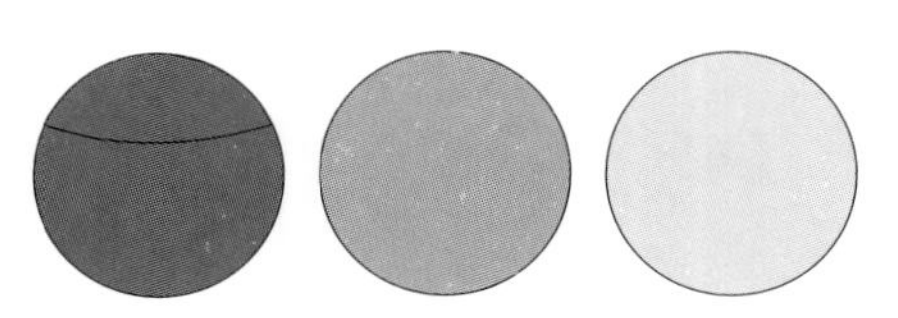

Black, Red, Green Circles
(Cut small section from Black Circle to place on Red Circle as Shown)

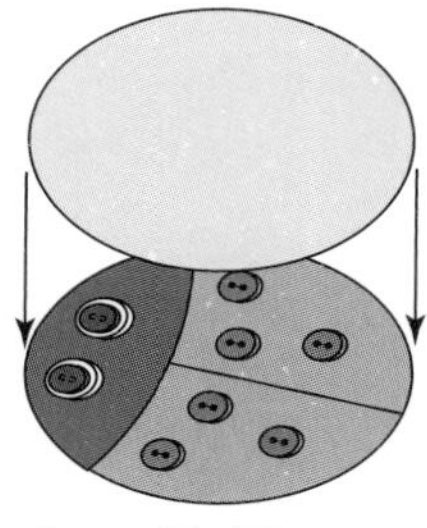

Assembly Diagram

# APPLIQUE PINCUSHION

**Ladybug Cushion**

Die cut three 5" circles (1 Green, 1 Red, 1 Black).
Cut the Black circle to fit the head.

ASSEMBLY:

Applique the Black head to the Red body.
Stitch a line down the center of the Red piece.
Sew 2 White and 8 Black buttons in place.
Sew Red/Black top to the Green tummy, with right sides together.
Cut a 2" slit in the center of the Green tummy.
Turn right side out. Fill with stuffing
Blindstitch the opening shut.

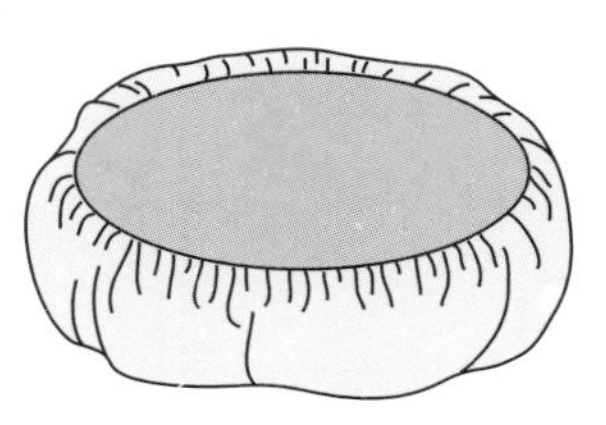

Large Tufted Cushion

Mini Hassock Tufted Cushion

# TUFTED PINCUSHIONS

**Large Tufted Cushion**

Die cut two 5" circles
Die cut a $2\frac{1}{2}$" x 44" side panel strip.

**Mini Hassock Tufted Cushion**

Die cut two 3" circles.
Die cut a $2\frac{1}{2}$" x 10" side panel strip.

ASSEMBLY:

Sew the ends of the $2\frac{1}{2}$" strip together, leaving a 1" opening in the center of the seam.
Gather the side strip (large cushion only).
Center and pin the panel to the edges of both circles, with right sides together.
Sew the edges of the strip to the circles.
Turn right side out through the opening. Stuff the cushion.
Blindstitch the opening shut.
Use a long needle to sew 2 buttons together with strong thread, going through the center of the cushion several times.

accuquilt®
better cuts make better quilts®

GO! baby®

# Mix & Match Quilt Dies

| fold fabric on one end |
| --- |
| to cut 2½" x 44" Strips |

GO! die #55014
Strip Cutter - 2½" (2" finished strips)
Includes seam allowance.

GO! die #55041
Fall Medley
pumpkin, leaf, acorn, large leaf

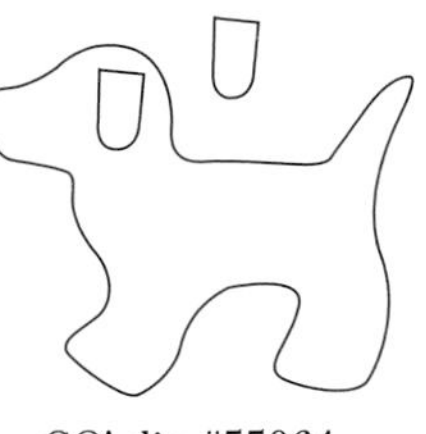

GO! die #55064
Gingham Dog

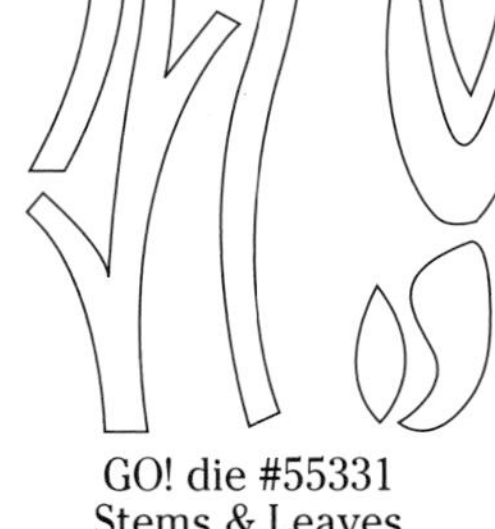

GO! die #55331
Stems & Leaves

GO! die #55334
Fun Flower

GO! die #55327
GO! Daisy

GO! die #55065
Calico Cat

GO! die #55328
Tulip

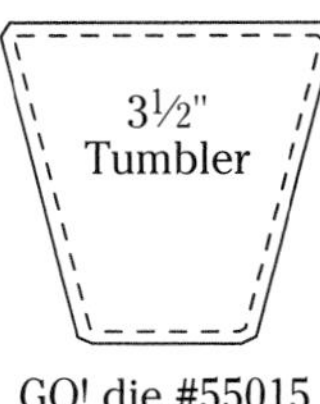


GO! die #55015
Tumbler - 3½"
Includes seam allowance.

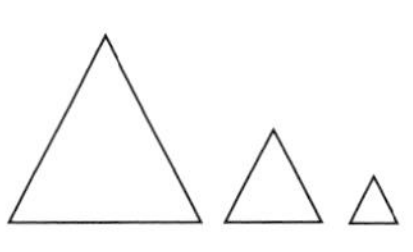

GO! die #55079
2, 1 and ½"
Equilateral Triangles

GO! die #55062
Overall Sam

GO! die #55061
Sunbonnet Sue

GO! die #55042
Funky Flowers

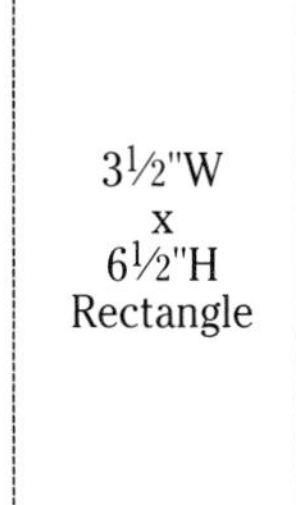


GO! die #55005
Rectangle
3½"W x 6½"H
(3"W x 6"H finished)
Includes seam allowance.

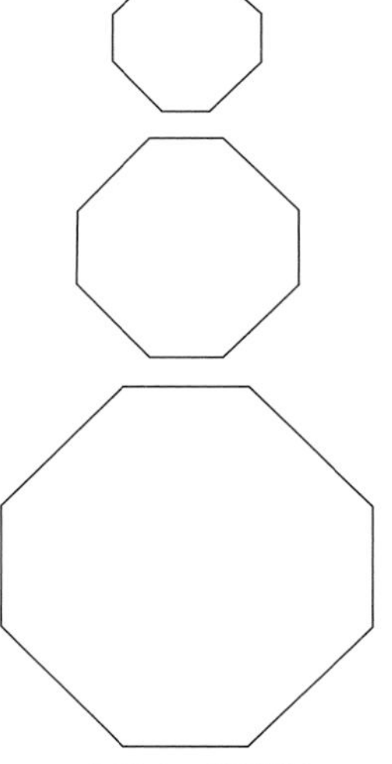

GO! die #55011
Hexagons - 2, 3 and 5"

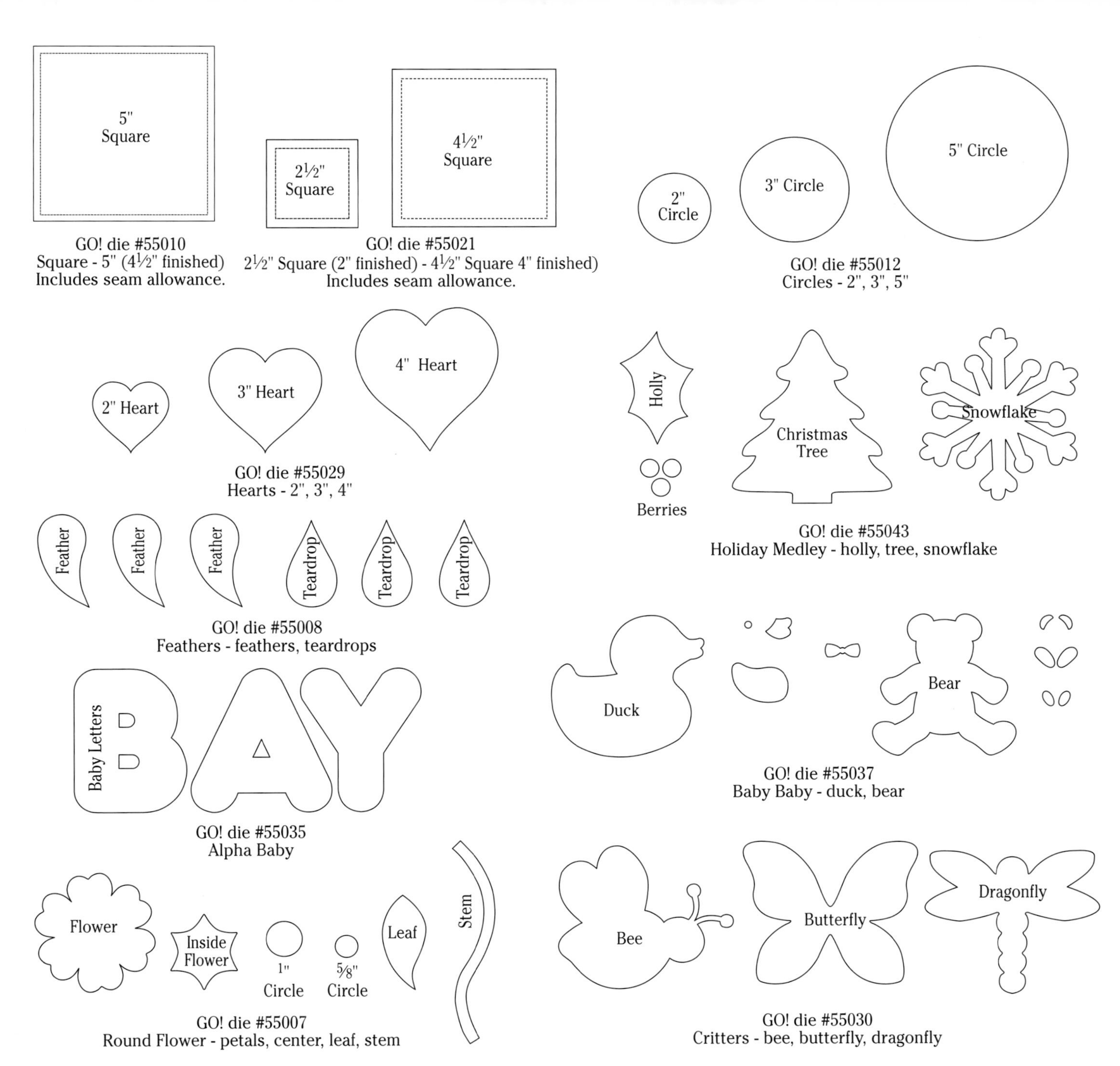
5" Square
GO! die #55010
Square - 5" (4½" finished)
Includes seam allowance.
2½" Square
4½" Square
GO! die #55021
2½" Square (2" finished) - 4½" Square 4" finished)
Includes seam allowance.
2" Circle
3" Circle
5" Circle
GO! die #55012
Circles - 2", 3", 5"
2" Heart
3" Heart
4" Heart
GO! die #55029
Hearts - 2", 3", 4"
Holly
Berries
Christmas Tree
Snowflake
GO! die #55043
Holiday Medley - holly, tree, snowflake
Feather
Feather
Feather
Teardrop
Teardrop
Teardrop
GO! die #55008
Feathers - feathers, teardrops
Duck
Bear
GO! die #55037
Baby Baby - duck, bear
Baby Letters
GO! die #55035
Alpha Baby
Flower
Inside Flower
1" Circle
5⁄8" Circle
Leaf
Stem
GO! die #55007
Round Flower - petals, center, leaf, stem
Bee
Butterfly
Dragonfly
GO! die #55030
Critters - bee, butterfly, dragonfly

*AccuQuilt® GO! baby*™ Fabric Cutter,
GO! die #55018 Value 4" square
GO! die #55012 Circles - 2", 3", 5"
GO! die #55079 Triangles
GO! die #55331 Stems & Leaves

PREPARATION FOR PILLOW FRONT:
Cut 12 squares, each 4"
(4 Teal, 4 check, 4 Tan)

PREPARATION FOR APPLIQUES:
Apply fusible web to applique fabrics.
Cut 1 Brown tail using the pattern.
Die cut all pieces:.

| | |
|---|---|
| Face | 1 Brown 5" circle |
| Ears | 2 Rust triangles |
| Eyes | 2 Gold small leaves |
| Nose | 1 Pink leaf (cut in half) |

ASSEMBLY OF PILLOW FRONT:
Sew 12 squares together. Press.

APPLIQUES:
Position and fuse appliques.
Stitch as desired.
Embroider eyes, mouth, and whiskers with floss.

**QUILTING:**
Layer backing, 1 batting, and top.
Quilt as desired.

CONSTRUCT THE PILLOW:
Insert a zipper between the 2 backs.
Trim to fit.
Sew front to the back, with right sides together. Turn right side out.
Stuff with 4 layers of batting.

# Purr-fect Pillow

*pieced by Donna M.J. Kinsey*

*A cuddly kitty keeps your favorite chair warm, waiting to welcome you home.*

SIZE: 12" x 16"

YARDAGE:
We used *Moda* "Antique Fair" by Blackbird Designs OR use the fabric colors of your choice.
1 Fat quarter each of Tan check, Tan print, Teal print, Rust print, Dark Brown print, Dark Brown, Gold, Pink

| | |
|---|---|
| Backing for Quilting | 15" x 20" |
| Pillow Back | 2 pieces, each 12½" x 16½" |
| Batting: | 2 yards of fluffy batting |

10" Zipper
*DMC floss* (Black, Pink, Green), chenille needle
*Steam-a-Seam 2* fusible web for appliques
Sewing machine, needle, thread

Pillow Top
Assembly Diagram

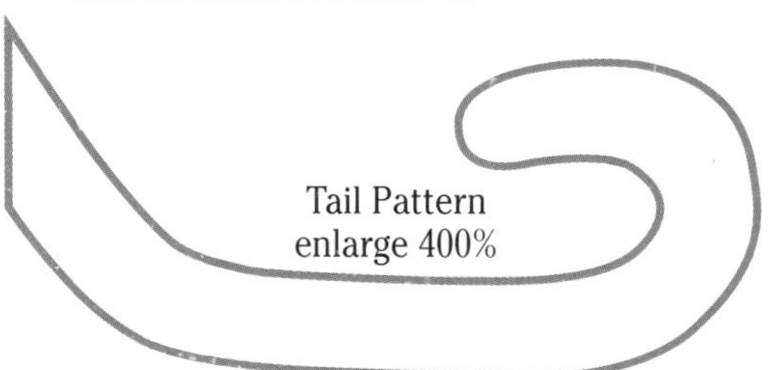